Breaking the Stained-Glass Barrier

Breaking the Stained-Glass Barrier

DAVID A. WOMACK

HARPER & ROW, PUBLISHERS
New York, Evanston,
San Francisco, London

FIRST EDITION

Designed by C. Linda Dingler

Library of Congress Cataloging in Publication Data

Womack, David A.
  Breaking the stained-glass barrier.
  1. Evangelistic work. I. Title.
BV3790.W56 1973   269'.2   72-11366
ISBN 0-06-069680-X

To BARBARA—
My Patient Wife and
Dedicated Missionary

Contents

1. A World to Conquer

PRINCIPLE: *The primary purpose of Jesus Christ in the world must never become a secondary cause in His Church.*

In the winter of A.D. 53–54, the apostle Paul and several of his associates departed from the city of Antioch and headed for the distant central highlands of Asia Minor. It was not the first time the Antioch Christians had said farewell to Paul, for this was his third missionary journey from their Syrian city. Eleven years before, he had gone out from Antioch on his first evangelistic tour with Barnabas and the young John Mark, and later he had traveled with Silas. Now he was accompanied by the half Jewish, half Asian-Greek Timothy and the Gentile Titus—strange foreign Christians who were themselves the products of Paul's far-reaching missionary ministry.

The evangelistic party followed the Roman trade route from Antioch across Syria and Cilicia, five hundred miles or more into the upper country of the Province of Galatia. There they were joined by Gaius of Derbe, and they visited Timothy's home area of Lystra and Iconium. Over the remainder of the winter they worked in Galatia and Phrygia to fortify the churches Paul had established on earlier journeys. Paul's historian, Luke, wrote of that trip, ". . . he departed and went over all the country of Galatia and Phrygia in order, strengthening all the disciples" (Acts 18:23). On his previous visits to this region, Paul had gone to the Phrygian cities of Lystra, Iconium, and Derbe, so the mention of Galatia probably indicates that the gospel had spread northwardly since his last ministry in central Asia Minor.

As the spring of A.D. 54 arrived, they moved to the west and came to the town of Metropolis, where they reached an important fork in the busy Roman road. Behind them to the southeast lay Syria and Palestine, and far along the other road was the fertile Tigris-Euphrates Valley of Parthia and the even more remote land of India. From Metropolis Paul and his group followed the road into the heavily populated Province of Asia, where they descended through river valleys to the city of Ephesus —economic and religious capital of the province and the gateway to the wealth and the wisdom of the East. Located at the heart of a large Greek-speaking population and constantly visited by travelers from all over the Roman world, Ephesus was to become a strategic Christian center from which the gospel would spread far and wide over the empire and beyond.

The story of the apostle Paul's evangelization of Ephesus and the whole Province of Asia is one of the most outstanding missionary accomplishments of history. If records were kept of all evangelistic triumphs, Paul's victory at Ephesus would still remain unchallenged, for by the end of a brief two years ". . . all they which dwelt in Asia heard the word of the Lord Jesus, both Jews and Greeks" (Acts 19:10).

Since the dawn of Christianity, the Church has been at its best when it has been the most militantly evangelistic. In those periods when it has made the greatest efforts to expand over the earth it has been refined by the most violent opposition. Such times of persecution have built into it a fierce dedication to take the gospel to every man at any necessary cost.

Unfortunately, the Church has never been able to maintain its most dedicated missionary enthusiasm over more than a few decades at a time. In contrast to its periods of greatness, the Church has been at its worst when it has failed to polarize public opinion about Jesus Christ, has retreated from the arena of open evangelism, and has closed itself behind the walls of its stained-glass sanctuaries.

Megalithic cathedrals, for all their aesthetic value, stand as sepulchral monuments to whole ages of religious feudalism, the crumbling remains of a sad era when the Church was reclusively introverted. Equally elaborate religious organizational structures have gathered about them their huddles of obedient serfs who ask only that the Church feed and protect them while they live and bury them securely when they die. Defensive Christianity places its priorities on visible symbols of power and invincibility, protected by its theological positions behind bulwarks of words, social orders, and claims to divine authority; while whole generations of unimpressed, uncommitted, and unevangelized people go by outside its unscalable walls.

The Church was never meant to be an impregnable fortress, out of reach of the common people. True, it was to be built on a rock, but it was to move out from its solid base of Christian security to proclaim the message of salvation to all men. It was not to be so much a depository of truth as a proclaimer of a heavenly message. It was not to be a far-off mountain hidden in clouds of mystery and religious awe, but an open plain made clear for all men in the light of divine revelation. The Church was to become an outgoing, proclaiming, evangelistic body of mutually loving brothers in Christ, dedicated thoroughly to the one all-consuming passion for the worldwide evangelization of the popular masses.

Jesus Christ commanded His Church to preach the gospel to every person in every ethnic society, but no generation of Christians has ever come close to fulfilling the Great Commission in its own times. Now, with the world's population at nearly 4 billion and growing at the alarming rate of 70 million people annually, the likelihood of evangelizing the whole world seems increasingly remote, at least with present methods and attitudes.

One of the most illustrative descriptions of the demographic explosion is an exhibit at the Smithsonian Institution in Washington, D.C. In an awesome display of white human skulls mounted on black cloth, the population scientists have shown that in Christ's day there were only about 300 million people on the earth. It was not until the first English settlers arrived in America, a millennium and a half later, that the earth's population first reached 500 million. It was another three centuries before the population had grown to 1 billion for the first time. Then, caught in the trap of his own productivity, man doubled his number in the next one hundred years, and in 1930 reached the astounding figure of 2 billion people. From the early Depression until the opening of the Space Age, man then added another billion to the score between 1930 and 1960. The following ten years produced another half billion persons. By the year A.D. 2000, the world apparently will have some 6.5 billion inhabitants, and demographic and ecological experts are saying we will enter the Age of Famines.

It used to be that the prophets of doom were the sidewalk preachers; but now they are the scientists. The apocalyptic climax of history once preached only in revival meetings and supported somewhat extravagantly with claims of divine revelation now is declared by the scientists with charts and carefully researched prognostications. It has become obvious that if the Church is ever to evangelize the world it must greatly increase its level of missionary activity and establish a broader base of operations very quickly, or else be forever too late to fulfill the Great Commission.

The Church, however, has a terrible problem. By some quirk in the evangelical mind many churches appear to be satisfied or at least willing to settle for a token presence in each country rather than a serious attempt to fulfill the actual commands of Christ. They rejoice over a few sheaves of gathered grain, while ignoring the massive harvest still standing in the fields. Their magazines and sermons abound with tales of missionary heroes, great personal sacrifices, and inspirational reports; but they never tell the American people that by and large the Church is only establishing a token presence in each land rather than a pervading witness. They do not say that missionaries often fail to reach the major cultural groups because they spend most of their time working with the more impressionable ethnic minorities who are seeking to improve their social status. Seldom do American contributors learn that much of their money goes into establishing Western institutions and funding a great many busy but not evangelistic activities, such as hospitals, elementary schools, orphanages, and other charitable works that in today's secular society can often be better sponsored by other agencies.

The Great Commission looms like a monolith above the religious horizon, challenging the Church to dedicate itself to the highest claims of the gospel. It must be understood that there is now no feasible way that the world can be reached by foreign missionaries alone; for even if the whole Church were suddenly to reverse its patterns of cultural isolation and make a serious attempt at total evangelization, we are already past the point of any possibility of making enough converts fast enough to evangelize the world by traditional missionary methods.

The only hope for the total evangelization of the world is to teach the Christian believers of each nation to evangelize their own people and to incite in each country the conditions in which spontaneous lay movements of church expansion may occur. In short, the Church must abandon its stained-glass sanctuaries and take the gospel out into the streets.

It has become clear to many who know the work of evangelical missionary ministry that the present degree of activity and accomplishment simply will not evangelize the world in this generation. There must be a radical change at every level of missionary endeavor if we are to take seriously the demands of the Great Commission.

For too long the work of foreign missionaries has been patterned after Western colonialism or else has built its methods on reactions to that historical period. Even the present emphasis on the establishing of indigenous churches came about as a corrective measure to offset the problems of paternalistic missionary methods. The Church ought to have been indigenously building upon the integrity of all believers from the very beginning, but so many activities were directed by foreigners and so many national believers were limited to unimportant and irresponsible tasks that some corrective measure became necessary. Therefore, there arose the emphasis on the indigenous-church principle that the national church should be self-supporting, self-governing, and self-propagating.

As the plan has developed, however, there are certain problems. In many countries the evangelical churches have fulfilled the basic requirements of the indigenous church plan, but still find themselves despairingly short of the total evangelization of their surrounding populations.

It is also possible for a national church to be fully indigenous without being based on other New Testament principles. For example, the Chinese communists adopted the indigenous church principle in their Three-Self Movement, which only led the evangelical churches astray from New Testament Christianity. The indigenization of the church is a necessary step in world evangelization, but it by no means includes all the needed factors for the fulfillment of the Great Commission.

It can safely be stated that no national church will prosper and grow at any realistic rate that is not founded on the indigenous church principle, set down so aptly by Melvin L. Hodges (*The Indigenous Church*, Springfield, Missouri: Gospel Publishing House, 1953) and other missionary writers. The missionary is a transplanted example of the Christian life; it is only as the native people of a land, endemic to their society and autochthonal to their culture, become active proclaimers of the gospel that there can be any natural church growth. A national church overly dependent on missionary leadership is like a wig—it looks as though it grew, but it is totally incapable of growing of its own life.

The indigenous church idea must not be seen as an end product of missions, but as a beginning base from which the real task of the Church may be accomplished. Much of the work of evangelical missions over the past decades has been that of repairing the serious mistakes of the previous hundred years. Now a fresh approach must be based on New Testament principles to make a serious attempt at fulfilling the Great Commission in our times.

What we need is a new matrix, a whole new way of looking at the missionary challenge. If our goal is to establish a token presence in each country, then we have already done quite well; but, if the Great Commission demands that every man, woman, and child on the face of the earth have a fair opportunity to accept or reject the gospel of Jesus Christ, then we are lagging almost hopelessly behind.

In search of a workable plan for worldwide evangelization, we must go back to the New Testament and base our global ministry on apostolic patterns and standards. To do this, we turn to the apostle Paul, who said, "I obtained mercy, that in me first Jesus Christ might shew forth all longsuffering, for a pattern to them which should hereafter believe on him to life everlasting" (I Timothy 1:16).

In the first century, the apostle Paul provided both a prototype for the modern missionary and a working model for a practical method of total world evangelization. His methods were especially observable at Ephesus, where after two years in that focal city in the Province of Asia, ". . . all they which dwelt in Asia heard the word of the Lord Jesus, both Jews and Greeks" (Acts 19:10). He not only reached the whole province geographically (*Asia*), but demographically (*all they which dwelt*) and culturally (*both Jews and Greeks*). He was not content with establishing a church in the Jewish subculture alone nor in planting a mere token presence of Christianity in Asia; rather, he effectively fulfilled the Great Commission for that time and place by carrying the gospel to all the inhabitants of the whole western sector of what is now the nation of Turkey.

Paul established a permanently successful church that was to be the center of the Christian faith over much of the next two centuries. Even though the apostle John was to warn the church against losing its first love, it would rekindle its flame and remain a burning candlestick for a very long time. In Ephesus would live the aged apostle John, and from nearby Smyrna would go forth the second-century missionary Irenaeus to preach the gospel in Lyons, France. The seven churches of the Apocalypse would be only a few of the many churches scattered all through that end of Asia Minor, and the New Testament letters to the Ephesians, the Galatians, the Colossians, and probably those of I and II Timothy and Titus were directed to this general area. Paul's biographer, Luke, said of the apostle's ministry at Ephesus, "So mightily grew the word of God and prevailed" (Acts 19:20). Whatever Paul did at Ephesus needs to be repeated again throughout the whole twentieth-century world.

To consider seriously a workable plan of evangelism we will examine the missionary ministry of the apostle Paul at Ephesus and apply the principles involved into a practical approach to modern missions. We will aim at a method and a way of thinking about Christian missionary endeavor that could saturate the world with knowledge of the gospel and establish a lasting evangelistic church of the dimensions demanded by the Great Commission of Jesus Christ.

When God created man, He said to His new creature, "Be fruitful, and multiply, and replenish the earth, and subdue it: and have dominion . . ." (Genesis 1:28). The task of primitive man was simple: He was to become the dominant life form on the planet. Now, with man walking on the moon, descending into the depths of the seas, flying at supersonic speeds through the atmosphere, doubling his total store of knowledge every few years, and even coming disturbingly close to reproducing living matter in his laboratories, we have abundant reason to believe that man has amply completed his first assignment. He has so thoroughly carried out his original task that he now has produced a terrifying ecological imbalance that threatens to destroy him.

With the coming of Jesus Christ, God gave a second commandment to man. This divine imperative is repeated in several passages of the Gospels and the Acts, for Jesus must have discussed it often with His disciples. The most commonly recognized statements are as follows:

All power is given unto me in heaven and in earth. Go ye therefore, and teach all nations, baptizing them in the name of the Father, and of the Son, and of the Holy Ghost: teaching them to observe all things whatsoever I have commanded you. (Matthew 28:18–20)

Go ye into all the world, and preach the gospel to every creature. (Mark 16:15)

Thus it is written, and thus it behoved Christ to suffer, and to rise from the dead the third day: And that repentance and remission of sins should be preached in his name among all nations, beginning at Jerusalem. And ye are witnesses of these things. (Luke 24:46–48)

Peace be unto you: as my Father hath sent me, even so send I you. (John 20:21).

It is not for you to know the times or the seasons, which the Father hath put in his own power. But ye shall receive power, after that the Holy Ghost is come upon you: and ye shall be witnesses unto me both in Jerusalem, and in all Judea, and in Samaria, and unto the uttermost part of the earth. (Acts 1:7–8)

The most prophetic of the Great Commission passages is in the Gospel of Matthew. The disciples had just asked Jesus, "Tell us, when shall these things be? and what shall be the sign of thy coming, and of the end of the world?" (Matthew 24:3). In a difficult passage in which Jesus mysteriously mixed the prophecies of the A.D. 70 destruction of Jerusalem with the predictions of the end times, the Lord said:

And this gospel of the kingdom shall be preached in all the world for a witness unto all nations; and then shall the end come. (Matthew 24:14)

With all due respect to the translators, the King James Version fails to include some implications in the original Greek text of this passage that have important bearings on any realistic consideration of its content. A more literal translation would be as follows: "And this Good News of the kingdom will be proclaimed (heralded) in the whole inhabited earth, resulting in a witness to all peoples; and then the end will have come."

Obviously, if the task of world evangelization is to continue until the end of this world order, then the obligation for proclaiming the Good News of the kingdom to the whole inhabited earth is still binding. The Great Commission has not expired, but is supremely applicable to this generation of massive population.

The New Testament emphasizes many complicated facets of Christian theology. However, in the Great Commission we are confronted with a disquieting simplicity. When it comes to the holy task of the Church, Jesus Christ calls for uniformity of action and singleness of purpose: true Christians are to go into all the world and preach the gospel to every living person in every ethnic society. It is a call to action, a command to total evangelization, and a commitment to proclaim the gospel to every man. The condition that must prevail before the close of the Christian era must be that all men in every ethnic society will have had a fair chance to accept the gospel of Jesus Christ.

The message preached by the first Christians was uncomplicated and direct. Jesus Christ, the Son of God, was crucified and buried; but the third day He rose from the dead. Forty days later He ascended to the

Father, from whence He would return for His Church. By the second century, it became necessary to state the gospel in an easily memorized declaration subsequently known as the Apostles' Creed. The present form of the Creed developed several centuries later, but its earliest known text said:

I believe in God the Father Almighty and in Christ Jesus, his only-begotten Son, our Lord, born of the Holy Ghost and of Mary, the Virgin, who was crucified under Pontius Pilate and buried; on the third day he rose from the dead, ascended into heaven, sitteth on the right hand of the Father from whence he shall come to judge the quick and the dead; and in the Holy Ghost, the holy church, the remission of sins, the resurrection of the flesh.

This simple declaration of the Christian faith did not reply to all the religious questions of man, but it did provide an easily understandable series of concepts for the evangelization of the popular masses. This central core of Christian doctrine—the gospel of the kingdom—would be universally applicable to all men, everywhere, in every culture.

The Christian justification for changing the religious beliefs and moral behavior of people in other cultures is so basic to Christianity itself that without it the whole of New Testament theology would be unworkable. The world evangelist must believe that Jesus Christ is the only way to God and that all other religions, beautiful and presently helpful as they may appear, are inadequate expressions of man's innate quest for God. Separated from God by his own sins, man rationalized his human state and invented substitutes for real communication with his Creator. Without a living knowledge of God, man degenerated into heathen cultures and false religions. Even though he covers himself with his cultural artistry and religious rituals, under the thin surface of his ceremonies lies the deep nostalgic melancholy of a lost child whose games do not satisfy his need for a real Father.

There are many biblical passages that describe the unique exclusiveness of Christianity. Jesus said, "I am the way, the truth, and the life: no man cometh unto the Father, but by me" (John 14:6). The apostle Peter said, "Neither is there salvation in any other: for there is none other name under heaven given among men, whereby we must be saved" (Acts 4:12). The primary motivation for world evangelization is love for our fellow men and the firm belief that all who do not accept the gospel of Jesus Christ are hopelessly lost and condemned to eternal separation from God. Christianity is by its very nature an exclusive religion. If Jesus Christ is right, then all the world must be evangelized and we must make converts among all other religions.

There are three words for "world" in Koine Greek—the one from which we get our words "geology" and "geography," the one that gives us the words "cosmos" and "cosmopolitan," and another one that is built on the Greek word for "house" and the word from which we get our word "remain." It is the latter that was used in Matthew 24:14, where it was translated "world" but means *wherever men dwell* or *the whole inhabited earth.* That phrase is followed by another that says the gospel will be a witness to all nations. The word translated "nations" is the one from which we get our word "ethnic," meaning peoples or ethnic societies. There can be no mistake about it; Jesus Christ intended that His Church should totally evangelize the whole inhabited earth, reaching into and pervading every ethnic society with the gospel of the kingdom.

The magnitude of the Great Commission is a frightening challenge to the twentieth-century Church, especially in view of the lack of missionary vision throughout most of the Christian era. We cannot answer for the ages that are past, but we are responsible for every man, woman, and child in every community in every cultural group of our generation. It is for today that we must answer to God; and if so we will have to develop a much more effective missionary program than we now have in operation.

As child-bearing was the commission of the pre-Christian age, so convert-making must be the goal of every healthy Christian congregation in this era. When a church's priorities are different from those of New Testament Christianity, it begins to withdraw from the world in cultural isolation and to fill an ecological niche provided by society rather than becoming a dynamic force for social and spiritual change. Furthermore, it begins to retreat from the stated claims of Christ by de-emphasizing original Christian doctrine, practice, religious experience, and priorities; and it replaces apostolic evangelism with charitable commitments and institutional efforts that may ease the conscience but do not evangelize the world. Eventually, it rationalizes its failure to evangelize by moving toward a doctrinal position of universalism with its accompanying complication of seeking to resolve differences and to find points of agreement with other liberal churches and even with the very non-Christian religions Christ told His Church to convert. Throughout history the process of syncretism has resulted mostly from the failure of competing religions to answer adequately the religious needs of men, thereby requiring a third faith to emerge out of the blending of two religions in trouble.

Much of the failure of the Church to make a meaningful impact on the world stems not so much from a liberal disinterest in the Great Commission as from an incomplete vision and inadequate methods. Many sincere Christians think well of the missionary cause, but fail to study the implications of the New Testament imperatives and thus do not take seriously enough the words of Christ. The actual conditions on most mission fields seem to indicate that by some common consent the evangelical community decided to be satisfied with a mere token presence of the Church in each country instead of an all-out commitment to total world evangelization.

As an example of this problem, the whole Christian church of all denominations in India makes up only 2.3 percent of the population after nearly three centuries of missionary activity and a much longer period of Christian influence, some of it going back to the first century. Unfortunately, the church in India has been strongly institutional and charitable in nature rather than openly evangelistic. As good as the contributions of dedicated missionaries have been, one would expect the thousands of past missionaries and the six thousand present ones to have made a greater impact on India. While one evangelical church has a total of 15,000 followers, the population of India is growing by 30,000 daily. This whole church is equal to one half-day's population growth in India!

The implications for the twentieth-century evangelical church are clear. If a Christian really believes that Jesus Christ is the only Savior, then he is morally responsible to share his faith and knowledge with all other men of his times. To do otherwise would condemn his own soul.

In the firm belief that many Christians, their churches, and their mission boards sincerely desire to fulfill the Great Commission in this generation, we will examine the missionary ministry of the apostle Paul at Ephesus in search of a workable plan of evangelism for our times. In the following chapters we will study step by step what Paul did at Ephesus and look for a series of missionary principles that can be applied to modern world evangelization.

2. Mapping Our Strategy

PRINCIPLE: *Evangelization on a worldwide scale requires preliminary planning and careful strategy. The planning is as critical as the execution in reaching the world for Christ.*

When the apostle Paul finished his successful ministry at Corinth and prepared to return to Antioch by way of Jerusalem, he began to formulate his plans for his third missionary tour through Asia Minor and Greece. His first contacts in these Greek-speaking Roman provinces had been mostly spontaneous, but now he would need to make a definite move to establish a firm base of Christian influence from which others could continue to spread the gospel over the whole region. He knew that a random scattering of churches would not be enough; there would need to be a Christian center from which large numbers of workers could be prepared and sent forth.

With his personal knowledge of the entire territory, Paul chose the city of Ephesus for its strategic location. Early in A.D. 52, perhaps in January or February of that year, Paul left Corinth and sailed across the Aegean Sea, accompanied by Silas and Timothy and a Christian couple named Aquila and Priscilla. Tentmakers by trade, the latter man and his wife had been exiled from Italy in A.D. 49 when Claudius Caesar "banished from Rome all the Jews who were continually making disturbances at the instigation of one Chrestus" (Suetonius, *Life of Claudius,* 25). If "Chrestus" was indeed Christ, then the Jews were exiled from Italy for anti-Christian demonstrations. Paul apparently had very good reason to establish a focal point for the rapidly expanding Christian Church.

The apostle Paul had chosen his strategic center well. Ephesus was a large city of some 200,000 people or more, and its annual Pan-Ionian Games brought twice that number for its May Spring Festival in honor of Artemis (Diana)—goddess of the hunt, the moon, fertility, and the protection of maidens. The Temple of Artemis was the largest building in the world at that time. Each of its 127 columns was 6 feet thick, and 37 of these columns had life-size figures at their bases. The altar was 20 feet square, and the building itself was 163 feet by 342 feet. The whole construction was built on an even larger foundational platform.

The goddess Artemis was the principal deity of the eastern end of the Roman empire, for in her Ephesian manifestation she was not so much the Roman Diana as she was the eastern Magna Mater—the Great Mother—who annually brought the god Adonis back from the dead, thereby ending winter and ushering in the fertility of spring. Artemis was not constructed of marble like the Western deities; she was built of wood with some part of her made of a meteorite that men had seen fall from the heavens (thus proving that she fell down from Jupiter). She was one of the most heathen of all the ancient goddesses, if there can be degrees of removal from non-Christian religion. She was like the grotesque images of India, only instead of having many arms she had multiple breasts for her fertility cult. At her base were many bees as symbols of her attending priesthood. A queen bee whose drones and workers served a vast region of fertility worshipers, she was a suitable adversary for the rising new religion of Christianity. Sooner or later, if the Church was to thrive in Asia, it would have to confront and defeat the Artemis cult of Ephesus.

The city of Ephesus was a center for commerce, learning, sports, and a particularly popular religion. Paul knew the importance of establishing a strong base at the very hive of Asian activity, so he carefully mapped out his strategy and initiated a well-devised plan.

In his preliminary trip to Ephesus, Paul wisely limited his activities to those he could realistically handle at that point, for he did not want to give advance notice to his future opponents. The Ephesian Jews were delighted to have such an enlightened scholar speak to them in their synagogue, and they "desired him to tarry longer time with them" (Acts

18:20). But Paul was only laying a foundation for his later ministry. He replied, "I will return again to you, if God will" (Acts 18:21).

Paul then left Aquila and Priscilla in Ephesus to prepare the way for his future plan, which he would not put into full effect for another two years. He sailed home to Antioch, traveling through Jerusalem to keep the A.D. 52 Passover.

The apostle Paul had a worldwide missionary interest, but he tackled that world one region at a time in a growing Christian witness. He chose strategic centers like Antioch, Philippi, Thessalonica, Athens, Corinth, Ephesus, and Rome; and he depended on the local Christians to evangelize their own surrounding territories. In the case of Ephesus, he selected an important population center from which he knew that there would result a spreading Christian witness over all the Province of Asia and out along the busy trade routes and shipping lines. He was prepared to take advantage of the local characteristics of the city because he took the time to study the region, make a preliminary planning trip, and leave people on the scene to do the first groundwork for the proposed evangelistic invasion of the city.

The greatest enemy of the success of Christian missions has never been the opposition of heathen cultures, but the lack of unified goals and the failure to plan strategically. Outside opposition and persecution have always driven the Church into a militant dedication to evangelism; but the failure to map out adequate plans for the future results in scattered efforts and ineffective methods. The task of world evangelization is so vast and close to the impossible that only the best coordinated and most thoroughly planned attack on the non-Christian world will offer any way to carry out the holy task of the Church.

Among missionaries there is a prevailing opinion that those who evangelize are not responsible for the results of their ministries, just so long as they faithfully reach the world geographically and continue to preach the gospel without compromise. Missionary stories often praise the pioneering veteran missionary who labored faithfully for many years without gaining more than a handful of converts. Such men really are heroes of a sort, often displaying the highest ideals of human virtues and in many cases even giving their lives for the cause. There are gravestones all around the world where missionaries have faithfully confronted heathenism with the claims of Jesus Christ. In the light of their great dedication and selflessness, one must weep for some of their ineffective methods and their failure at their primary task of pervading society with the gospel. The common sentiment that the way a person fights the battle is more important than the outcome cannot apply to Christian missions. We are commanded to make converts, to disciple all nations. Any methods that do not produce a growing, thriving church are absolutely inadequate in the light of our fundamental responsibility.

There are seasons to the harvest. When Paul found a city that was not ready to listen, such as Athens, he moved on to another place like Corinth where the field was ripe. He did not run from difficulty, but he placed his priorities on strategic locations, planned his moves in each area, and did not waste his time on antiquated methods or unworkable ideas.

The concepts and methods of evangelical foreign missions have developed slowly since the Reformation. At first the efforts were largely those of individual missionaries who were awakened to the needs of the world. Later, missionary societies and denominational boards began to serve as sending and supporting bodies for these missionaries; although the actual work on the foreign fields continued to be almost totally individual. To this day the pattern is very much the same. Mission boards go into great detail to recruit and screen missionary candidates and raise the funds to support their foreign ministries, but the missionaries themselves are sent out without sufficient training beyond the levels of personal motivation and survival, and they arrive in foreign lands without a unifying strategy or any specific practical methods to make their churches grow rapidly enough for any realistic progress.

There must be more than a general, idealistic missionary interest if the Church is to evangelize the world in this generation. Our missionary purpose must be defined and applied in specific plans and workable methods, complete with preliminary strategy and preparatory activities.

There must be a prevailing global goal, shared by individual missionaries, evangelical mission boards, and the whole Bible-believing community. The chances now for ever attaining the master goal are so remote that only a unified philosophy of missions and a cooperative and well-planned effort will accomplish the task.

Because of the great variety of Protestant missions, it will be impossible for all groups to work together in close harmony. There are too many philosophical and doctrinal differences to unite them successfully in their foreign work. Such unity is not to be desired, for few groups adequately stress all facets of Christian truth. By and large, the various Christian churches form a sort of ecological balance, each group developing different sets of Christian characteristics that somehow add to the understanding of New Testament revelation or serve to counterbalance certain extremes and excesses. Where one group would strongly emphasize the need to popularize theology for the common masses, another would stress the need for deep theological training for Christian leaders. Both of these concepts are necessary. They are not mutually exclusive ideas, yet seldom exist side by side in the same group. Where one denomination stresses the security of the believer in Christ, another emphasizes the need for daily holy living as a prerequisite for heaven. If the extremes of either case were true, the whole Church would be in terrible trouble; but the fact that two branches of Protestant theology counterbalance each other adds to the overall depth of the Christian experience and keeps either branch from toppling the whole tree.

Even though variety and differentiation are characteristics of any living entity, there is a tremendous need for evangelical groups to meet together and map out a realistic strategy for missions. The present level of scattered and undirected missionary efforts simply will not come anywhere near the demands of Christ for our times. Given agreement on the basic ideas of the lostness of sinners and the salvation of Christian believers, these evangelical groups should be able to agree also on missionary methods and a prevailing strategy. The evangelical denominations should complement one another in their foreign missions programs, while still retaining their separate identities; for more can be accomplished through such differentiation than by uniting into a single body.

Some fine efforts are already being made toward such cooperation. The Evangelical Foreign Missions Association (EFMA), connected with the National Association of Evangelicals, and the Interdenominational Foreign Missions Association (IFMA) have made good progress in uniting the concepts of their member groups. Some of the members of the World Council of Churches, although diluted by the syncretism of the Ecumenical Movement, have continued to be evangelical in their general outlook. However, many groups in the latter organization have majored on social problem solving and on theoretical discussions rather than a concern for the application of Christian missions to the realistic spiritual needs of mankind.

Although most missionary activities of all Christian groups continue to be largely individual efforts within an unguided and unplanned context, some groups are beginning to see the need for better missionary strategy. There have been some interdenominational evangelistic efforts, particularly in large citywide or nationwide campaigns. The immediate reports of such joint efforts have been good, but some of the long-range results have shown them to be a shallow overrunning of the land rather than in-depth evangelization. Mass evangelism is meaningful only when converts are oriented to the life of local Christian communities of believers. Joint campaigns have the distinct disadvantage of de-emphasizing the importance of local congregations and of trying to lay aside differences between groups. The kind of cooperation that is most needed is not that of joint campaigns, but of complementary activities and mutual respect. If two groups are working effectively in the same community, they should not limit one another on the basis of some kind of territorial rights, nor quarrel over the same people. They ought to realize that they will appeal to different people at various social levels and that they can both work wholeheartedly at their major tasks without opposing one another.

However, some kind of notice needs to be served. It must be recognized that some groups will adopt apostolic methods and grow rapidly,

while others will cling to traditional and outmoded ideas that still continue out of the Reformation and paternalistic colonialism. Such churches will not grow to any effective degree in today's world. The growing
young churches cannot afford to slow down their programs or limit their
own expansion just to keep peace with those who hold to antiquated
methods. The evangelical community must be allowed to grow freely
and spontaneously, with no territorial limitations placed by its own
supposed brothers. There certainly are enough barriers to world evangelization without having additional ones placed by the Church itself.

There is great need, then, for preliminary planning and careful
strategy on the part of missions leaders. Without a pervading purpose
and a strategy for carrying out that purpose, missionaries will continue
to scatter their efforts over a wide terrain without really fulfilling the
demands of New Testament Christianity. They need this kind of guid-
ance not only to accomplish the missionary task through well-planned
methods, but to eliminate nonproductive work. In view of the urgency
for getting ahead of the population growth in pagan areas, even normally
worthwhile activities must come under scrutiny for their relative contributions to the primary task and their current priority.

Group A sent a missionary couple to a city to establish a ministry for
its church. Rather than study the national language in a special school
for that purpose, these missionaries went directly to the country and
attempted to learn the language while beginning their work. For a while
the man attended the national university to make contacts with the
students; but his conservative views and linguistic inadequacy only separated him from the predominantly radical students. The man withdrew
from the university and rented a house in a very poor suburb of the city,
where he began to hold services in his living room. His wife was fairly
good with Sunday school stories, having taken a college course in the art
of the flannelgraph, so they began to reach a few neighborhood children.
Four years later, they returned to the United States with the report of
a little congregation of thirty people, mostly women and children, whom
they left in the care of an independent missionary with a similar record
of failure.

Group B sent a missionary couple to the same city the same year. The placement of these people on that field was part of an organized plan to evangelize the country by establishing the mission's churches in strategic locations. The couple was prepared in specialized missionary training in America and sent to a language school to learn to speak fluently before attempting to work with the people in the target area. When they arrived on the field, they joined a well-prepared team of missionaries who knew why they were there and what they had come to do. By teaching national believers to evangelize their own nation and carefully studying the living patterns of the population, they soon had churches springing up spontaneously within their chosen regions. In four years their group grew from a little handful of believers in two or three churches to more than five thousand members in eighty churches and other preaching points at various stages of development. When they returned to the United States for a year of fundraising, there was a continuity in the churches because other members of the missionary team and a growing army of trained national ministers would carry on the activities. While in America the couple would receive further orientation.

The advantages of preliminary planning and strategy are obvious when we look at missionary work over a period of time and compare the results of different approaches. Little such study occurs because we seldom look at the greater picture. By spending our time in day-by-day problem solving and fundraising we fail to realize the general ineffectiveness of much that goes by the name of evangelism. Furthermore, the geographical removal of missionary work from the location of most missionary leadership allows ineffective people and inadequate methods to prevail undetected over long periods of time.

Unorganized and unplanned efforts offer no possible solution to world evangelization. Missionaries must be trained in proper missionary methods, languages must be learned, cultures adopted, societies identified with, and meaningful dedications made if the world is to be evangelized in this generation. Sincere as missionaries may be, even the most devout efforts are meaningless if the overall plan is not part of a total strategy.

The people of America may be impressed by great missionary stories of bravery and dedication, but yet not know if effective work is being done unless the missionary is part of a larger plan. It is not enough to send out missionaries and support them and their work; we must send out teams of prepared missionaries who will apply a workable plan of evangelization to strategic areas of the world.

The only remaining possibility for world evangelization in our lifetime is to teach the Christian believers of each country to evangelize their own people and for missionaries to create and take advantage of the conditions in which spontaneous lay movements of church expansion may occur. The relationship is somewhat analogous to that of a shepherd who seeks good pasture for his flock and tries to protect the sheep from predators, but recognizes that the task of lamb-bearing rightly belongs to the sheep. Until missionaries and their sending boards realize the principle of this simple lesson—that the role of missionaries is to create the conditions in which the national church will multiply spontaneously and develop to healthy maturity—there will be no significant advancement toward the objectives of the Great Commission.

Mission boards and the whole evangelical community must analyze their purposes and set a worldwide strategy for their missionaries. We may also ask that the local missionaries plan for the most effective use of their personnel and the most strategic centers for their work. The very concept of making a preliminary study of a field and following it up with a well-organized plan will revolutionize much of the present missionary activity. The cooperative unity that comes with studying a field together will in itself improve the quality of the work, even if other factors are less than optimal.

Given a group of missionaries working within a general plan and dedicated to a well-organized and rapidly growing church in their field of responsibility, the question is the selection of the most promising locations and the best plan of action. Inasmuch as most of the remainder of this book will investigate the apostle Paul's methods, we will concern ourselves at this point with the choice of practical locations.

The first step is to define the relative density of population in various parts of the country and to determine the patterns of social movement. For example, let us examine a hypothetical country, which like ancient Gaul is divided into three parts. There is a coastal plain, a mountainous zone, and an inner grassland plateau. The capital city with its industrial complex is on the coast, where also are located a number of secondary cities and towns, surrounded by widespread vegetable farms. In the mountains there are various mining operations and little towns enclosed in narrow valleys. Most of the mountain people either work in the mines or grow small crops on the slopes and the fertile valley floors. These farmers tend to come from families who have lived in the mountains for a long time, while the miners mostly have migrated from other parts of the country. The inner plateau is composed of grasslands suitable for animal grazing, plus tropical growth along the rivers. Although the grasslands are the least populated areas of the country, they also do not provide much work for the rising generation of more education-conscious youth. The cattle and sheep raisers of the region hire some of the young men, but the rest must look for work in the mountain mines or in the industries and small farms of the coastal plain.

Into this country comes a team of missionaries who have determined to set up a national evangelical movement that will come to the attention of the masses and produce a strong national church. There are other Christian groups at work in the country, but they make up only a mere 3 percent of the population, mostly in the capital and made up of foreigners and people who have attended mission schools. New Testament Christianity is not a movement in the country. In fact, the existing churches are not progressive and have not increased in a long time.

Upon studying the social movements of the country, the missionaries discover that, although the higher density of population is in the capital and its surrounding towns of the coastland, the greater movement of people is related to the mines. Many of the mine workers spend their lives in the mountains, but there is also seasonal and short-term work that brings people in from the coast and the plateau for a few months at a time. Many men work in the mines just long enough to gain sufficient money to buy a farm or start some small business elsewhere.

The missionaries decide to start churches in all the main mining centers so that the converts will carry the gospel back to their homes all over the country.

Next, they decide that the movement of workers from the plateau to the coast comes through three major routes through river valleys and mountain passes. They choose locations where these travelers generally spend the night, and they establish churches there. Thus, they not only locate on the main routes of demographic movement, but approach the people at a time when they are most susceptible to new ideas.

Once these strategic locations have been determined and churches established there, other churches will spring up spontaneously wherever the converts carry the gospel. The missionaries will have to coordinate their efforts very well to keep up with the natural growth of the church.

This was just one way to interpret the data and get started. As in the game of chess, there are many openings with almost limitless variations. The important thing is that these missionaries put a workable plan into effect and cooperated well to make it effective.

At this point, the missionaries can easily become so busy with the growth of their predominantly rural church that they will neglect the evangelization of the cities and towns. Some of the growth from the mountains may develop churches in the urban areas, but they will be made up mostly of unsettled, lower-income people. The missionaries will make an important decision to plan a major church located in a main transportation center of the capital city. As much research must go into the location of this church as went into the planning for the rest of the country. This evangelistic center should be large enough to give some social status to the movement, while serving as a motivational and training center for the other churches and gospel workers throughout the country. Never should it be allowed to compete with the rest of the movement. Here the church can hold its national conferences, and from it the national ministers and missionaries can launch their major evange-listic campaigns.

From the very beginning the planning group will work toward the establishing of fifty or more smaller churches scattered all through the capital and its surrounding towns, so the church will start a number of outstations where the believers will hold services under the auspices of the mother church. Soon this approach in the capital will spread the movement to other coastal towns and back into the mountains and plains where the program began. There is still much work to be done. There are programs to initiate and national people to train. Even with this oversimplified view of a planned approach to the country, however, one can see that these evangelical missionaries are in a fine position for potential growth and the possible fulfillment of the Great Commission in that land.

The patterns of other countries will be different from those of the field we have just examined and not nearly so easily identified. In some cases, a rapidly expanding capital city may be the place to begin. In others the best place may be in a busy seaport. The important point is to locate the centers of activity in places where the natural movements of the population will carry the gospel where the missionaries want it to go. This was why the apostle Paul chose Ephesus, because any idea that would catch on there would be carried far and wide. He chose the one city in Asia where the efforts of a limited team of missionaries could effect a large area of land and population.

In most countries the setting up of a workable strategy will be complicated by the years of previous missionary work and the patterns already established with the national believers. A willingness to change and the courage to face up to past failures will make the difference in the future effectiveness of the mission. The most devastating problems come from attempts to salvage past errors and to defend subjectively the traditional programs into which so many men have poured their lives and dollars. However, we must face up to conditions as they actually are and analyze our progress realistically in the light of well-planned research. Even under the worst conditions of negative public sentiment, a mission can reverse its procedures and develop a growing movement again. Public opinion is a fickle thing, not nearly so rigid as the programs of the mission itself.

Every culture is different, and the people within it respond at different rates and in different degrees. An evangelistic campaign in Brazil would be expected to gain several hundred converts at the very least, while a necessarily less public effort in Iran would probably not see more than five or ten people express a genuine interest in conversion to Christianity. The success or failure of the churches in each country must be judged by the conditions in each place and not by the work occuring in other countries or cultures. Evangelism has its seasons when the popular masses are in stable or unstable periods of their national lives. The criterion for judgment should not only be in the rate of conversions but also in whether the missionaries and national ministers are taking full advantage of the opportunities before them. The strategic planning of missionary efforts must take into account every possible factor and then move with decisive courage to take advantage of all favorable conditions.

The key to good missionary programing is well-researched preliminary planning with a workable strategy that is easily understood by the local believers and spectacular enough to come to the attention of the masses. The basic requirements for successful missionary work are a strongly motivated sense of cause and a burning passion for world evangelization focused keenly on a purposeful plan of operation. Missionaries must constantly keep in mind that in reaching the world for Christ the planning is as critical as the execution. Any attempt to go directly to the task without such preparation and preliminary activities will only lead to eventual frustration and failure.

The population of the world is growing too fast and the Church is too far behind in the race for any kind of unplanned evangelism to approach the objectives of the Great Commission. Evangelical missions and their missionaries must coordinate their efforts through effective planning and careful strategy if they are to take the gospel to their world.

3. A Team Concept of Missions

PRINCIPLE: *The apostolic pattern of evangelism re-quires the teamwork of dedicated people laboring effectively toward a single prede-termined goal.*

Although the apostle Paul was one of history's great individual personalities, he never chose to work alone. Throughout his career, first as an active defender of Judaism and later as a devout apostle for Christianity, he always surrounded himself with capable people who shared his dedication and willingness to work. His letters to the churches abound with the mention of his friends, with whom he shared the responsibility and the credit for the accomplishments of their mutual labors.

At Antioch, Paul worked with Barnabas and other local men of God, and on his first missionary journey he traveled with Barnabas and John Mark. On his second trip he began with Silas (Silvanus), but soon added Timothy and Luke. Titus was also one of his earliest companions, for he went with Paul to the Jerusalem council in A.D. 49. At times some of Paul's co-workers would remain behind, as in Macedonia, but later would rejoin him at another place.

When Paul sailed into the mouth of the Cayster River for his first look at Ephesus in A.D. 52, he had Silas and Timothy with him, as well as Aquila and Priscilla. Luke had stayed at Philippi to care for the new church there. Aquila and Priscilla would now remain in Ephesus to prepare the way for Paul's arrival in that city in the spring of A.D. 54. Their contribution at Ephesus may be compared to that of John the Baptist before the ministry of Jesus, for those whom they taught learned the ideas of John the Baptist as a preparatory course to Christianity.

Two years after his preliminary planning trip, Paul and his group came across the "upper coasts" or highlands of Galatia and Asia and settled at Ephesus for a major evangelistic campaign. Although Luke did not mention whether Aquila and Priscilla were still there when the group arrived, Paul sent greetings from them in his First Epistle to the Corinthians, which he wrote from Ephesus in A.D. 56. Little is known about this couple after the Ephesian campaign, except that they had a church in their house at Ephesus and later did the same at Rome. When Paul wrote his Epistle to the Romans, they were already in Rome, for he said, "Greet Priscilla and Aquila my helpers in Christ Jesus: who have for my life laid down their own necks: unto whom not only I give thanks, but also all the churches of the Gentiles. Likewise greet the church that is in their house" (Romans 16:3–5).

When Paul arrived in Ephesus, he had with him an active team of Christian workers. Timothy, Titus, Gaius, Erastus, and Aristarchus certainly were with him, for they are mentioned either in the Acts account or in the epistle Paul wrote from Ephesus. Apollos and Sosthenes joined him later from Corinth. Luke may have come down from Philippi, for his knowledge seems to indicate his personal observation. If Aristarchus was there, then Secundus may also have come, for both were Thessalonians. This being the case, Sopater of Berea might also have come. Tychicus and Trophimus appear to have been Ephesian workers who developed early in the campaign. The movements of these people are impossible to trace, but the evidence is strong that Paul arrived in Ephesus with a team of missionaries, who later were joined by other workers to form a powerful group who would work together for the evangelization of the province.

The team apparently was mobile, with many comings and goings over the whole region. It appears that Paul's helpers may have worked the countryside and other Asian cities in addition to their labors at Ephesus, while Paul himself remained mostly in the central city. In one case, Paul sent Timothy and Erastus on a special assignment to Macedonia. Perhaps on the same journey Timothy went as far as Corinth. Titus also traveled to Corinth, bearing the epistle to that city.

It is important to note that these workers were responsible to Paul.

This was no scattered effort, but a well-planned and well-executed campaign of evangelization and church establishment. Paul was definitely in charge of the whole operation, for Luke said, "So he sent into Macedonia two of them that ministered unto him, Timotheus and Erastus; but he himself stayed in Asia for a season" (Acts 19:22). All the evidence points to an active team of responsible missionaries evangelizing a whole region in a coordinated and cooperative effort.

The principle of responsible teamwork must be applied to modern missionary efforts if we are to escalate our evangelization into a worldwide lay movement of spontaneous witnessing. At the heart of the movement there must be a very efficient, well-coordinated group of men who know what the task is and how to go about accomplishing it. They must be movers of men, experts in the molding of public opinion, and exceptionally convincing witnesses themselves.

As great as some individual missionaries have been in the past, we need to recognize that more cooperative efforts on a larger scale are long overdue. However, this concept of team missions goes contrary to much of the prevailing ideas of missionary work today, for those who most influence missionary thought are not necessarily those who are its most active or its best practitioners. Sad but true, the work of some famous missionary individualists made better books than it made national churches. Great individual efforts are still required, but they must be coordinated with the work of other equally dedicated people, both missionary and national, and they must be made within the framework of a broader context. The great missionaries of the future will be those who learn to view the world largely outside the frontiers of their own personal limitations and who can incite successful missionary activity in an expanding number of other people. One man with the right concepts can multiply his own effectiveness if he can pattern a thousand witnesses after him. In the new context of missions, the missionary must be a man of unusual personal vision and industriousness who can inspire other people and reproduce in them the same vision and zeal for hard work that beats in his own life.

When I was a missionary in Colombia, I learned rather quickly the necessity of teamwork. I was raised and educated on the concept of great missionary loners, but I could see no way that mere personal sacrifice, suffering, or exemplary patience could accomplish the task I envisioned for Colombia. I had ruled out martyrdom as a method rather early, although being stoned a few times and arrested for preaching where Protestantism was forbidden did gain me some small recognition among the national believers. My letters home to my supporting churches contained true accounts of my adventures in dugout canoes on the Arauca River, wading to my knees in mud in the Sarare jungles, and fording piranha-infested waters in the Amazon Basin. I was making converts and encouraging national pastors, but I could see no way that my level of missionary work could ever evangelize the country.

Perhaps the most frustrating part of my missionary work was that of the Bible school, where we attempted to train national ministers. A whole staff of missionaries was assigned to teach for six months of each year. At one time I was teaching twenty-nine hours a week in addition to being the national treasurer, the pastor of a small church for which we had no national minister, director of several grade schools, and general missionary with the duty to travel among the churches. We had a good missionary team, but we were all working too hard and putting a lot of effort into a largely unprofitable task. Our students were not the kind of people who would ever be able to make an evangelistic impact on the country, but were mostly barely literate rural boys. The country people could leave their crops for a few months, but the city folks could not afford to be gone from their jobs even for a day. Our whole student body numbered fifteen! It was clear that we would need a whole new pattern for our work if we were to produce a growing church in Colombia.

While the missionaries were struggling with the Bible school and failing to provide competent workers for the urban areas, we had two city churches in Bogotá that were trying to grow in spite of the lack of new workers. Through a series of events including missionary furloughs and other factors, Harry Bartel and I and our families were left as the only missionaries in Bogotá for about a year, and we had to take the leadership of these two growing churches. We had to postpone the Bible school until we could bring our missionary staff back up to a practical level. The idea of missionaries pastoring churches is opposed to the traditional view of the indigenous church principles, but the Bible school had produced no possible pastors at that time. We had one Colombian minister with any advanced training, and he had gone to America for further study. We decided we would make the most of it and give the Colombian pastors examples of pastoral leadership. We were to learn a tremendously important lesson: that missionaries must not only push national workers into ministry, but must show them the way through responsible leadership.

One day, Harry and I stood on top of Mount Monserrate and looked down on the city of two million people spread out a thousand feet below us. With the din of the city in our ears, we divided Bogotá down *Calle* 26 and each took the challenge of a million Colombians. It was a moment of idealistic abandon, but we came down from the mountain with our targets well defined and our plan of action quite clearly in mind. Harry was in the north side and I in the south. Within a few months our churches were growing very rapidly, each of us preaching to several hundred people in every Sunday service.

Our goal was not to build two growing churches larger necessarily, but to incite an evangelistic movement that would spread over the country of its own fervent vitality. In each church we developed teams of gospel workers who would hold outstation services in various places outside the church on Sunday afternoons. The congregations would generally not return home after the Sunday morning services, but would go out in responsible teams to distribute literature, hold evangelistic services in homes and in the open air, and make the gospel a public issue in the city. Sometimes they would be attacked, for those were violent days in Colombia. At times they would have their Bibles taken from them and burned in the streets. Occasionally someone would be arrested. In spite of the persecution, they multiplied very rapidly and seemed to thrive on the opposition. One of the outstation workers declared after a particularly rough situation in which fifteen believers had been attacked by several hundred angry people, "Wherever they throw rocks at us, we will take those rocks and build a church!" There developed such a high intensity of enthusiasm that our city workers soon began to go out on weekends to witness in the surrounding cities and towns of that Andean savannah.

The churches became centers of a wide range of activities, including elementary schools, a method of rehabilitating converts from among alcoholics and complicated marital situations, an aid program for feeding and clothing new converts from among the poverty classes, and other such services, in addition to all the religious activities. Social help was in every case considered a temporary measure, for converts were expected to become responsible, hard-working citizens of their community, capable of assisting the next converts who would follow them. The people gladly tithed 10 percent of their income to the church, knowing that their money was going to the central cause of their lives.

Our congregations grew faster than we could train teachers to instruct them. Because of his limited building, Harry had to go into a construction program to renovate an old plastics factory, but he would often preach to five hundred people or more and at the dedication of the new church we crowded nearly 1,800 into the building. I was regularly preaching to 800 to 1,000 on Sunday nights, and on special occasions we put loudspeakers outside and managed as many as 1,500. The greater work, though, was being done by our outstation teams, which between the churches were preaching to 3,000 to 4,000 people every week.

When missionary Verlin Stewart and his family returned from their furlough in America, we started night Bible schools in the two churches to train these active workers who were already so involved in city evangelism. Immediately, we had over sixty students, and these inspired people became the key to the present growth of the Assemblies of God in Colombia. Soon we were able to open the main Bible school again, this time with a different kind of students and a larger number enrolled.

Today most of the sites of our outstations have become churches. Most of the pastors of those churches are former team leaders, and each of their churches now has its own circle of new outstations that in turn will become churches with their own pastors. Even the present national superintendent, Gustavo Quiroga, was one of the first outstation leaders. Another team worker, named Gonzalo Quintero, now pastors nearly 2,000 people in the city of Neiva. The Bible school continues, training students who have already been involved in successful mass evangelization before attending school for their formal ministerial studies.

The people who are evangelizing the country today are the Colombians themselves. The missionary staff is larger than it has ever been, because a rapidly developing national church requires more missionaries for a variety of coordinated activities and a wider geographical spread; but the church has become a living entity that grows of its own vitality and momentum. The turning point came when we developed teams of responsible Christian believers and sent them out in an organized and effective pattern of activities, backed by two churches that were rapidly coming to the attention of the community. As the missionary staff grew, it also continued in a dedicated teamwork, well coordinated with the goals of the national church.

While I was pastoring in Bogotá, a sociology major from the National University began to attend the meetings to do research on me and to write a paper for his class. He observed our programs at the various levels of social and spiritual ministry, but he was most impressed by the militant evangelistic teams. When he had finished his paper, I asked him what he had decided I was. He grinned and said, "I know what you are. You're a Protestant agitator!"

He was right.

This is exactly what today's missionary must be—an agitator of evangelistic action! He must be a precipitator of religious crises! He must incite the conditions in which widespread evangelization will occur by inspiring cooperative team efforts of militant evangelism among national believers. He must create a prevailing attitude of intense dedication to the cause of Christ in which the believers will be ready even to die for this cause. The problem is that most missionary work—like much pastoral work today—is far too casual ever to fulfill the Great Commission even locally, far less on a worldwide scale. The gospel of Christ must become a public issue, and the churches must be well organized to take advantage of every opportunity.

We must somehow remove the competitiveness from Christian ministry and replace feelings of mistrust and petty jealousies with a deep dedication to the primary task of the Church. Pastors working in the same city or country need to operate as a unified team. If there are similar congregations in a large city, they should meet together and map out a strategy for the total evangelization of their communities and act like a team rather than argue over territories and members. It is not unrealistic to consider that there can exist a similar church for every five thousand inhabitants of an area, in addition to other less similar churches. If there are 100,000 people in a community, there can be twenty similar churches, many of them growing to 500 or more in attendance without reaching any saturation point. When one considers the great number of unevangelized people in the world, the very idea of church competition becomes a ridiculous game played by men with limited vision.

The greatest enemy of church growth is not the presence of another similar church in the community, but the low levels of organization and intensity of religious enthusiasm within the church. If people are excited about their church and are given a practical and well-planned way of reaching their community without embarrassment, the church will grow. The same principles apply to a region, a province, a nation, the world. For any activity that involves numbers of people, team action is superior to even the greatest individual efforts.

Let us apply some of the principles of team action to the problems of church growth. It is a well-recognized fact that churches tend to level off at different numbers of people in attendance, and that there is a direct correlation between the size of the church and the kind of local organization and mobilization of members. These same factors apply both on mission fields and in America, for the problems are universal.

There are many churches with 35 to 45 in attendance, but there are relatively few in the 50's, 60's, or 70's. Then, there is a large number of churches with 85 in attendance. These seldom have less than 80 or more than 95, and the golden number of 100 evades them year after year. For some reason, there are few churches with 110 or even 115, but there are many with 125 to 135. The next group clusters about the 165 to 185 level; and there is another group with 250 to 275. After that, the numbers are less predictable, but there are some that cluster about the 325 figure, and others stop just short of 500. The next group is at 700, and others grow to just under 1,000. The number 1,200 is the next one to beat, but few ever do. There seems to be a barrier of some kind at about 1,185 where the church has to become some kind of huge corporation to keep growing.

It is very unlikely that any church will grow past the number of people that its pastor can care for efficiently. Simply stated, a church will grow to a point just short of its pastor's inability to tend to his flock. He can extend his own limitations by improving his depth of experience and education, preparing better sermons, organizing his time more efficiently, and generally being nicer to people; but he will eventually find a level beyond which he cannot increase his capacity by self-improvement alone. He must begin to build a team of competent staff members who extend his limitations by the added factors of their ministries. In most cases, however, the limitation level will not be multiplied by the number of workers, for most pastors do not choose strong enough men for their associates, thus building into their programs yet another limitation factor that will sooner or later slow down the church growth again.

The pastor of a church of 35 people in attendance is generally trying to do the whole task by himself, plus holding down a secular job to support himself and much of the finances of his church. Most of the 35 people are related and attend the church to escape the larger crowds in bigger churches. It is very difficult to get new converts to join such a group, so the growth above 45 is some kind of miracle. At about 50 people the one-family characteristic begins to break down, and new people can more easily be assimilated into the group. The pastor starts to use his people more effectively, and they begin to believe that their church can grow beyond the tiny church level. They grow into the 80's in attendance with little difficulty once they get the concept of being a full church with a wide range of activities.

It must be understood, though, that the present church pattern is not the only alternative to spreading the Christian message and caring for congregations. The early Church had no large church buildings, but met in homes scattered all through the community. If the Church is to be centered in buildings, then those buildings should come to the attention of the masses and the congregations should grow to a size to make some sort of favorable impression on their society. There is one characteristic of the Church in all ages: it must either progress and grow in numbers and maturity or else fall backward. Like mountain climbing, there is no reasonable direction for success but up.

There are certain characteristics to the church of 85 in attendance. The pastor is still doing most of the public work. His is often the only voice heard from the pulpit on Sunday, and he does most of the other work of the church. He may have departmentalized his Sunday school, but he teaches the adult class himself. It is very hard for new leadership to form among the laymen because the pastor sees their rising involvement as a threat to his own authority and leadership. The musical program is very casual, relying mostly on unplanned presentations. The majority of American churches, and many of the foreign ones, are in this category because of the general quality of ministerial training, which offers much for preaching content but almost nothing for church administration and the involvement of laymen into active teamwork.

The pastor with 125 in attendance has learned something that the one with 85 does not know. He has surrounded himself with a team of people who work with him at some degree of efficiency. There is a church secretary, so that the people of the community can call the church at any normal business hour. The church is putting out a good bulletin and letters to the members and new converts; and there are adequate records to show the pastor, the board, and the staff members what is going on. There is a choir that practices for the Sunday services. The pastor does not have to do everything himself, but can rely on the help of the people whom he has trained. He can give full time to the ministry and less to the physical details of the church. The pastor with 125 faces another problem—whether to build a larger church. Typically, he is about to build a new sanctuary to seat 500 people. This will give him another limitation factor, for there is nothing that will slow down church growth like an empty barn of a building. People are attracted by crowded sanctuaries, not necessarily comfortable ones. Most pastors would do well to go to double services long before they plan to build new churches. Of course, a church will not grow beyond its normal seating capacity, so eventually it must build; but it should stay functional in its architecture and stay within the ability of the congregation to support construction without limiting evangelism. The name of the game is people, not real estate.

The same patterns of growth continue through all the clusters of churches at different numerical sizes. The growth of the church is determined by the organization of the congregation and its comparative intensity of enthusiasm and meaningful activities, plus the current level of competence of the pastor and his staff. As a pastor learns to mobilize his people into an efficient team, gains some insights into a more inclusive organization, and discovers new ways to maintain group involvement and intensity of congregational feeling over a longer period of time, he will see his church expand. Eventually it will slow down and stop growing again until some new factors are introduced to change the limitation barriers.

The range of church sizes from 35 to 1,200 in attendance is not a steady slope, but a staircase. Each step requires an increased involvement of the laymen and more efficient teamwork of a pastor and his staff. There are exceptions, of course, but there would be few churches with more than 85 people if these factors were not true. There appear to be barriers, or steps, at 45, 95, 145, 200, 290, 350, 500, 700, 1,000, and 1,185. The last one is something like the sound barrier, after which a whole new set of rules apply. One, for example, is that a larger congregation must form smaller units within the greater mass of members if it is to maintain growth. A church of over 1,200 becomes a small subculture in the society, and is subject to all the dynamics of such social groups. In most cases, it is wise to break such a church into two or more congregations.

The figures would vary for every country according to the culture, but much the same staircase of growth-limitation barriers occurs for any context of church expansion. If we are to reach the world for Jesus Christ, then we must apply these same principles of church growth to widespread evangelization. The growth of a church on the mission field will meet the same kinds of limitations among a group of missionaries as the American church finds in its pastors. At first, they try to do everything themselves; then they eventually learn that it is only by motivating leadership in others that the national church will grow. Later, they find that they must involve a greater and greater number of workers in the leadership of the ministry, and that these workers must be trained for leadership on a widening scale. There is a direct relationship between the growth of the church on a mission field and the missionaries' own ability to mobilize the lay masses into efficient teams of capable Christian witnesses.

Have we not reached the time when specialized teams of evangelistic missionaries could go into certain areas for two years or less to help get struggling or beginning churches off the ground? In most places, the first stages of church growth are the hardest, because there is nothing there to attract the public or even to come to the attention of the masses. Such teams could give the resident missionaries and national ministers a boost over the difficult levels of church growth by organizing such activities as house-to-house visitation and literature distribution, witnessing, evangelistic campaigns, effective follow-up procedures, and other helpful ministries that the local missionaries might not have time to develop.

The apostle Paul knew that it was not enough simply to put Aquila and Priscilla in Ephesus; he had to hit that area hard with a whole team of well-oriented workers. Such an approach could greatly strengthen the Church in many places, although the local missionaries and pastors would have to be prepared to make the necessary adjustments in their own ministries to keep up with the expansion. As we have intimated in this discussion, a growing church is something more than adding numbers; it is a whole complex of expansion of ideas, attitudes, vision, organizational concepts, and faith in what is not yet seen. Big churches require big men to lead them. The fact is that the numerical growth is a result of the other more complicated growth patterns. If a church has 85 members, it must start to act like 125 before it will ever see that many people. And, if a national church has 2,000 believers, it must begin acting like 4,000 before that number will appear in its annual report.

Many Americans associate foreign missions with the highest ideals of human life. However, life on a pedestal is both unrealistic and generally untrue. Most missionaries are extremely practical people who live in constant contact with the most basic realities of human existence. They rather enjoy their pedestal occasionally, but they spend most of their time surrounded by the grossest darkness, the most depressing poverty, and the most desperate depravation. Most of them are so busily engaged in the minute details of daily living that they fail to look on the greater field and see the need for better patterns of work.

Take two American Christian families and put them in a foreign city with a strange culture and an even stranger language. Ask them to raise up a Christian community of believers who will spread the gospel all over that city and its country in a mighty wave of inspired, militant evangelism. All day every day they work at the task, fighting a thousand devils every time they try to accomplish anything, and facing apparent failure to communicate every time they open their mouths. The convert they thought could become a pastor turns out to be a polygamist, and the Bible says he should be the husband of one wife. The girl they thought could be a secretary for the Bible school is pregnant by an unidentified father. The city traffic is unlike anything they can describe in their newsletters. Somebody in America sent them a box of candy, and they have to fill out a dozen government documents in as many offices to get it out of customs.

Now, put those same two families together in a missionary meeting where they are supposed to plan the evangelistic strategy for their city. Likely, they will use their brief return to the English language and their contact with their own peer group to vent their frustrations, sometimes on one another.

Due largely to this syndrome of missionary behavior, the history of missionary cooperation and teamwork is rather sad, to say the least. The beginnings of missionary teamwork will not come from leaving the planning of such cooperative efforts to the discretion and instigation of local committees of missionaries. The mission board itself needs to have a pervading philosophy of group missions and must train its missionaries in such methods before they ever leave for their foreign labors. A new concept of missionary work must be taught in evangelical colleges to produce people with team mentality, for it is only as missionaries form such interrelated methods of working that there can be the kind of church expansion necessary for the completion of our total task.

By the time a missionary leaves America for his field, he should know how he is to fit into the existing team in the country of his destination. He should know to whom he is responsible for his work and how his ministry relates to the work of the other missionaries. If he is to work in a Bible school, he needs to know what his relationship is to the other staff members and what his personal responsibilities are. How does the Bible school program relate to the work of preaching missionaries who are involved in mass evangelism? How does the literature work coordinate with the Bible school and the mass evangelism? What is the philosophy of the missionaries for working with the national church leaders? These and many other questions should be answered early, or else the missionary team will produce scattered and unrelated results and eventually limit the growth of the national church.

Built into the very fabric of all missionary activities are the strengths and weaknesses that ultimately will determine the quality and the growth of the national church. Unless the team works correctly from the beginning, the missionaries will one day find that they have dedicated themselves to a minor skirmish instead of the great battle. Then, about the time they think they have done all that is possible for foreigners to accomplish in a difficult situation, someone else with a better-organized team will come to do a better job. We must never convince ourselves that our members are so thoroughly converted and so spiritually motivated that they will never turn to another cause or another church. The best of men will abandon a sinking ship. We must maintain our growth or else decline; it is a law of church expansion.

In this business of world evangelization, we set our own goals and lay our own limitations. The sad fact is that much more has been said to missionaries about having the faith for great goals than has ever been said of having the faith and the qualifications to work for these goals in a dedicated teamwork with other equally devoted missionaries. How difficult it is for great men to work together; yet, it is generally their ability to cope with the problem of teamwork that allows them the luxury of greatness.

In a typical instance, a mission field is opened by one or two missionaries who spend most of their time establishing churches in strategic locations. Later there will be other missionaries to enlarge the team and increase the activity of the national church. One couple could continue to develop country and small-town churches. Another could be in charge of following up the spontaneous churches begun by the believers as they move about the country and settle in different places. Yet another missionary couple might lead a mass-evangelism program to hold campaigns in the cities and towns to bring the church to the attention of the public. Still another could develop an evangelistic center in a main city to provide a place for conferences and to create a certain status with the wealthier classes. Probably all of the missionaries would teach in the Bible school, possibly located in one of the secondary cities; but one of the missionaries would devote full time to directing the ministerial training program. There would be other programs that would need their own staffs, such as correspondence courses, literature production and distribution, radio and television communications, and other advanced programs. In fact, the larger the ministry grows in that land the more teamwork is required.

Each of these missionaries would be very busy in such a program, but his work would be interrelated with that of others and in some important way would contribute to the whole operation. Depending upon many intangible factors, this national church would probably grow to about 10,000 believers with this kind of organization before requiring a restructuring of its base. One of the most questionable factors would be whether the missionaries would be capable of developing an equally motivated and equally well-organized team of national pastors and administrators. The secret of growing beyond the barrier of 10,000 would be the ability of the missionary and national leaders to foresee the limitations and to take the necessary steps to mobilize a wider group of leaders. Here they must battle the tendency of leaders to try to maintain themselves in office and to hold the status quo. If leaders view the rising workers as a threat, the growth of the church will eventually stop; but if they will motivate young men to strive for excellence and deep devotion to Christ and His cause they will see continued expansion. An expanding church requires an expanding leadership, and any attempt to limit the rise of new leaders will also limit the growth of the church, much as stunting new corn will diminish the abundance of the harvest.

Even though many human frailties plague church leadership, a proper administration and a definite chain of command are absolutely essential to world evangelization. The work must be so organized that each missionary has an unlimited opportunity for progress within his own scope of duties; but it is just as important that he be answerable for his ministry and responsible for his results. Every person along the chain of administration must be accountable to someone.

The apostle Paul was definitely in charge of the operation at Ephesus, for the other members of the team "ministered unto him." Evangelical mission societies differ in their internal structure, but the factors of responsible leadership of leaders and of answerable accountability of missionaries must be present.

The lack of proper supervision and responsible teamwork is one of the major problems of foreign mission work. Missionaries are scattered over so many countries and located in such widespread areas that close supervision is nearly impossible. That is why the mission's administrative body itself must have definite guidelines for the missionary to follow and by which he may evaluate his own progress. He must know what his job is, how to go about it, and how to determine whether he is getting it accomplished. Then he must be able to fit his work into the progress of his fellow missionaries for a total impact on his country and the world. Only good leadership and inspired teamwork can ever achieve such a goal.

An apostolic approach to world evangelization requires the teamwork of missionaries and the unification of ideas that come with responsible leadership. Jesus said that the harvest is great but the laborers are few. This being the case, we must make optimal use of our limited manpower by mobilizing our missionaries to the finest degree of their efficiency and by motivating national churches to cooperative team evangelization. This is the only way that we can avoid the limitations that can slow our progress and curtail our growth.

4. The Formation of a Nucleus

PRINCIPLE: *Before an evangelist can take the gospel to
the masses, he must first form a nucleus of
properly oriented believers with whom the
new converts may identify.*

When the apostle Paul and his team of evangelists arrived in Ephesus, the first thing they did was to form a nucleus of believers who represented in microcosm what they wanted the greater church to become in all of Asia. This preparatory step to mass evangelization was very important to them for two reasons: (1) the basic concepts of Christian doctrine, religious experience, practice, and priorities must be emphasized from the very beginning so that apostolic standards will be held in their authentic relative respect; and (2) the new converts must find an existing body of believers whom they may emulate and with whom they may identify.

Luke said that Paul began with a group of twelve Ephesians who had already been taught the doctrines of John the Baptist. We may assume that this important groundwork was laid by Aquila and Priscilla, who had been busily preparing the Ephesians for the arrival of Paul's evangelistic team. In addition, these people had sat under the eloquent teaching of Apollos, an Alexandrian Jew who was "mighty in the scriptures." Luke said of him, "This man was instructed in the way of the Lord; and being fervent in the spirit, he spake and taught diligently the things of the Lord, knowing only the baptism of John" (Acts 18:25).

Aquila and Priscilla apparently took advantage of the arrival of this teacher by leading Apollos into the Christian faith and then working with him to prepare these twelve Ephesians for the coming of Paul. Luke said, "Aquila and Priscilla . . . took him unto them, and expounded unto him the way of God more perfectly" (Acts 18:26). By the time Paul and his team arrived in Ephesus, Apollos was gone on to Corinth, but he later joined Paul in Asia and worked with him for the evangelization of the province. Aquila and Priscilla remained in Ephesus and had a church in their home. It was not until some two or three years later that they returned to their city of Rome and started another church in the very heart of the empire.

There is some indication that Paul was surprised that Aquila and Priscilla had not led these twelve people into full Christian conversion, for his first question to the twelve was, "Have ye received the Holy Ghost since ye believed?" Apparently, the Judeo-Roman couple had followed instructions, though, for their conversion of Apollos was proof that they were acting with deliberate purpose.

When the Ephesians admitted that they were acquainted only with the teachings of John the Baptist, Paul explained to them that repentance for sin is insufficient for salvation, but that one must also have a living faith in Jesus Christ as the Son of God, salvation being both a corrective and a constructive measure in the human life. The twelve accepted the teachings of Christ willingly, and "were baptized in the name of the Lord Jesus."

Having brought them into Christian conversion, Paul then returned to his original subject and laid hands on them to receive the baptism in the Holy Spirit. The result was that "the Holy Ghost came on them; and they spake with tongues, and prophesied" (Acts 19:6).

Paul and his team members must have smiled as they listened to the twelve Ephesians speaking with other tongues and praising God. It was as it had been at the Day of Pentecost and at the home of Cornelius, the same as it had been wherever the gospel of Christ had been established and had grown. These men knew no other Christianity than that which Jesus had founded and which developed in the human life with these Pentecostal characteristics. The seed of Christian life was growing again, this time in the heart of the cult of Artemis.

Now that Paul had a properly oriented nucleus of Ephesian believers

—saved, baptized in water, and filled with the Holy Spirit—he was ready to launch his evangelistic campaign on the Province of Asia.

For any purposeful mass movement among lay people there must first be a central control group to determine the eventual characteristics of the mass. It takes only a little yeast to make bread, but the growth of that active control factor determines the whole texture and ability to rise of the otherwise inactive dough. In another context, Paul said, "Know ye not that a little leaven leaveneth the whole lump?" (I Corinthians 5:6). So also the evangelization of a mass of people requires a nucleus of Spirit-filled, thoroughly convinced believers who become activists among the people and provide the patterns for the masses to emulate.

In any effort to establish a growing movement, the leaders must constantly keep in mind the rather complicated characteristics of group dynamics. People in groups do not think the same as do individual persons. Single individuals can at times be reasonable and even logical; although allegiance to a researched and thoroughly logical system of thought is rare in so-called *homo sapiens*. Man the wise rarely exhibits the wisdom for which he has named himself. The result is that he acts often in an irrational way and seldom experiences those special insights into his own behavior that bring order into his otherwise chaotic existence. This is not to deny rationality, but only to admit that much human behavior is based on general impressions about life and its experiences rather than specific knowledge and subsequent logical thought patterns.

There is, in fact, considerable discussion today among social scientists as to whether man is a rational being at all. Some say that man has few instincts, but bases his behavior on reasonable choices that he has learned to make through the sum total of his experiences. This school of thought considers man to be a rational creature who acts on the basis of reason and is responsible for his own deeds. The other end of the spectrum on this subject considers man to be irrational, a victim of his own subconscious drives and chemical complexity. These say that human life is a series of blind reactions to incomprehensible stimuli; while the proponents of rationality say that life is a chain of conscious choices for which the maker is responsible whether for good or for evil. The question is: Does he act out of conscious will or unconscious intuition?

The argument for rational choice versus inner complusion is in itself absurd. The complex creature we call man is his own worst argument for his own highest qualities. He is at one and the same time both logical and illogical, both rational and irrational, both capable of incisive clarity of thought and of blind bondage to his own subconscious drives. He is God's greatest miracle, this mass of chemical components and portable organic plumbing who deigns to scan the heavens and reach out his hand to his Creator. A strange mixture of terrestrial life and cosmic intelligence, he reacts to his environment in an earthly, chemical way; but the wonderful faculties of his amazing mind lift him above the other life of this planet and make him a unique creature capable of Godlike reasonableness and clarity of thought.

The best argument for the irrationality of man is his chemical nature —the fact that a spurt of adrenalin into his bloodstream can produce a predictable behavioral response. At the same time, an equally positive argument for rationality is the minds of the men who are capable of studying such reactions and writing about them. We must conclude that man is often irrational, usually random in his choices, and seldom logical; but that he is nonetheless capable of rational choice and therefore responsible for his actions.

Man is at his reasonable best when he can express himself as an individual within a context of orderly presentation. However, when he forms groups of people, his whole complex of rationality changes. Small groups can have the same characteristics as individual persons, but only as the social structures of such groups allow individual expression and extend the particularities of individual minds into a group context. Eventually, though, the members of a group will categorize their thinking into neatly labeled compartments and rally their loyalties around some of the more vocal or influential members. This is a good reason for Christian believers to be vocal witnesses in their communities, for some followers are almost certain to develop from any polarization of human thought.

Masses of people are not logical at all, but behave in response to the acceptance or rejection of symbolic images. The masses think intuitively and collectively, not logically and independently. Here one must exercise some caution, for people in normal control of their faculties blend into the masses at different degrees at different times. For most people, the mass psychology is only a willing lapse of individual response. Single persons can fade in and out of mass thinking, thereby keeping some control of a sort of intuitive logic. Few people know when they are being rational or irrational, but they do have certain inhibitions and prejudices that tend to regulate their society. The absence of this quality turns the mass into a mob.

The dynamics of a large group is extremely complicated, but the Christian evangelist must at least keep in mind that masses of men must have symbols around which to build their structure of prejudices based upon their favorable or unfavorable impressions of things. Before the Church can grow within such masses, it must become an issue in the community and become subject to the public's irrational scrutiny and search for meaningful symbolic images around which to rally its loyalties. If the verbal imagery of the Church can capture the capricious allegiance of the masses, it can then sort out the individual persons capable of further training and bring them into the whole depth of Christian theology and ministry. If the Church is to have any chance of reaching the masses, it must recognize the characteristics of group behavior and work with the world that is, instead of with an imagined effectiveness in a world that never was. We must accept the fact that there is a fundamental difference between Individual Man and Group Man.

Jesus gave us good examples of this distinctive feature of man. When preaching to the masses, he spoke in parables and illustrated His messages with practical applications to human living. Mark said, "And with many such parables spake he the word unto them, as they were able to hear it. But without a parable spake he not unto them: and when they were alone, he expounded all things to his disciples" (Mark 4:33-34). Jesus created His own public image as a Teacher and Miracle Worker before He declared Himself as the Incarnate Son of God. He did not ask the masses to reason with Him, but gave them symbolic images in the form of parables, which they could accept or reject without having to go through the paths of reason. Only with the inner group of disciples and with individuals did He expound the implications of His public preaching. He recognized that there are two kinds of people—the sometimes rational and the mostly intuitive—and he worked with them accordingly. He made a difference between sheep and shepherds and between the harvest and the harvesters. Matthew records, "But when he saw the multitudes, he was moved with compassion on them, because they fainted, and were scattered abroad, as sheep having no shepherd. Then saith he unto his disciples. The harvest truly is plenteous, but the labourers are few; Pray ye therefore the Lord of the harvest, that he will send forth labourers into his harvest" (Matthew 9:36-38).

The apostle Paul also recognized the problem of communication with the masses. He knew that he would have to form an original nucleus of properly oriented believers as a pattern for the Ephesian church. Around this nucleus of enthusiastic, militantly evangelistic prototypes he would build an expanding mass of followers that would eventually number in the millions. Yet, those millions would still retain the characteristics of that first control group.

It is interesting to note the parallel between the opening of the Ephesian church and the original church in Jerusalem. Both were preceded by the teachings of John the Baptist, perhaps as a necessary conceptual bridge between Judaism and Christianity. Certainly the ideas of personal guilt and repentance as opposed to religion as a communal or national activity must come before Christian salvation is possible. Both Ephesus and Jerusalem had their twelve men for a nucleus of believers; and both cities had their Pentecostal experiences of being filled with the Holy Spirit and speaking with unknown tongues. On the Day of Pentecost the apostle Peter preached to the multitudes that gathered, and at Ephesus the Spirit-filled people prophesied in their own language under the inspiration of the Holy Spirit. In both cases, the baptism in the Holy Spirit was a necessary antecedent to mass evangelization.

Let us examine what Paul actually accomplished with his Ephesian nucleus of believers. First, he insisted on right apostolic doctrine by leading the people beyond the teachings of John the Baptist into a full revelation of Christian truth. He did not allow the ideas of the Church to blend with the people's previous religious concepts in a syncretistic union, but prescribed that the purity of Christian doctrine should prevail from the beginning.

Second, Paul also insisted on right apostolic practice, for he did not accept non-Christian baptism. After inquiring about their beliefs and leading them into full Christian conversion, he baptized them in water according to the Christian formula. In search of a modern baptismal formula, it is important that we use the words taught us by Jesus in Matthew 28:19: ". . . baptizing them in the name of the Father, and of the Son, and of the Holy Ghost." Paul's baptizing "in the name of the Lord Jesus" only indicated the difference between Christian baptism and that of John.

In the apostolic Church there were no baptized and unbaptized Christians, for all Christians were baptized soon after conversion. It must be remembered, though, that Paul worked in a context in which the time of genuine conversion was apparently clear. In some cultures an affirmative response does not indicate conversion, so missionaries must allow a probationary period for the indoctrination and change of lifestyle of the potential new believer. It should be noted that wherever baptism in water has been treated casually as an optional practice the identification of believers with the Church has been extremely weak. The apostolic context of Christianity demands baptism as a necessary practice, for it both identifies believers with the Church as a symbolic death to past life and resurrection to new life, and provides a visible image for the influencing of the masses. Baptism is a willful act of the convert to publicly forsake his previous life and to dedicate himself to the new matrix of Christian life.

Third, Paul insisted on right apostolic experience. He first asked the Ephesians if they had received the Holy Spirit, then he laid hands on them to receive the experience. As on the Day of Pentecost, they were filled with the Spirit—an experience that was evidenced by the phenomenon of speaking with other tongues and prophesying.

Fourth, Paul insisted on right apostolic priorities. He put first things first by establishing his nucleus on a firm spiritual foundation before attempting to communicate with the more volatile masses.

This combination of apostolic doctrine, practice, religious experience, and basic priorities continued to characterize the Christian Church throughout the first few centuries until it became so blended with Greek and Roman mentality and practices that it lost much of its earlier purity and vitality. That first kind of Church was the one established by Jesus and taught to the world by His apostles. If ever there was a right kind of Christianity, then that must have been it. Otherwise, the standards of the true Church would depend too much on human wisdom and the decisions of earthbound councils. One must decide whether the true Church comes by divine revelation or by historical development. If it is by divine revelation, then today's Christianity should make every possible effort to return to the standards of that first apostolic Church. Today's ineffective evangelization and the claims of the New Testament itself make it quite clear that only a full return to the doctrines, practices, religious experiences, and priorities of the apostolic Church will offer any real hope for reaching our world.

Paul obviously placed great importance on whether the Ephesians had been baptized in the Holy Spirit. He straightforwardly asked them, "Have ye received the Holy Ghost since ye believed?" By this, he implied that the baptism in the Holy Spirit is an experience that they should have known whether they had received or not, and that the occurrence of this experience was subsequent to initial belief. It was evidenced by speaking in previously unlearned languages and expressing inspired utterances of praise to God and admonitions in one's own language.

Like salvation and water baptism, the infilling of the Holy Spirit belongs to the whole Church. Any attempt to return to the religion of the apostolic period would be incomplete without it. Yet, it is perhaps the least understood and most criticized of the apostolic experiences.

Some denominations have emphasized the baptism in the Holy Spirit and identified with it, and an increasing number of people in the old-line denominations are discovering the blessings of this apostolic phenomenon; but its first-century nature and the emphasis placed on it by Christ and His earliest followers rightly keeps it in the proper domain of the whole apostolically oriented Christian community.

Only eternity will reveal the tragedy of medieval Christianity. The Church began with a beautiful simplicity of design and singleness of purpose that somehow became confused and conceptually polluted. Christian doctrine was dogmatic in nature and could not long survive the dilution of syncretism with Greek philosophy and polytheism, and with Roman legalism and social structure. When Christianity became the official state religion of the Roman empire in A.D. 325, it was inevitable that the great number of unconverted and uninspired "Christian" citizens would destroy the life of that first unique form of militant Christianity, for real spiritual life cannot exist by man's official decrees or be maintained by governmental order and supervision. The true Church continued for a short while in reclusive monasteries and isolated towns, but it could not long survive removed from the arena of human conflict.

The real hero of the Reformation was the Bible. Once the printing press began to put Bibles into the hands of the common people again, it was inevitable that men would insist on a return to the wonderful Church described in its pages. If there had not been a Martin Luther, there would have been someone else to raise his voice and call for New Testament standards. Step by step, with its progress retarded by the slow rise of literacy in the Western cultures, the Church rediscovered justification by faith, salvation as a definite experience, and the relationship of holy living to spiritual progress. Personal commitment to Christ and His gospel replaced Christianity as a dominating cultural force, and evangelism as a method of expansion replaced Christianization by military force. Today the Church is still in the process of rediscovering that original life of apostolic Christianity; for the current revival of first-century characteristics in many of the liturgical and Reformational churches, including the much-publicized charismatic renewal, is certainly an encouraging sign that apostolic Christianity may yet blossom on the earth.

One manifestation of this return to apostolic Christianity is the Pentecostal Movement, which began at the turn of this century. At the time, the Protestant churches were unprepared for such an event, engaged as they were with the issues of liberalism brought on by reactions to higher criticism and the developing of the new notions of evolution and psychoanalysis. The churches were too busily involved with attacks from the outside to concern themselves with this apparent deterioration of traditional Christian experience from the inside. They dismissed the tongues-speaking people as hysterical fanatics and dropped them from their memberships, not taking the time to listen to what the new Pentecostals were really preaching. The churches took issue with the Pentecostals for calling themselves "full-gospel" Christians, not realizing that what they were calling for was a full return to the whole apostolic gospel. There were many excesses, brought on mostly by their forced separate identification from the rest of the evangelical church; but when the confusion finally cleared away and the world began to recognize them as evangelical believers, the Pentecostals had already formed well-organized churches and were spreading over the earth at an amazing rate of growth. As in the case of Jesus' acceptance by the existing religious structure, the stone that kept getting in the way turned out to be the chief cornerstone. The movement that was dismissed as too fanatical turned out to be a revival of apostolic standards and the key to the evangelization of the world. The Pentecostal Movement should never have been forced to develop its own organizations, but the irrepressible urge to world evangelization that accompanies the baptism in the Holy Spirit could not wait for the eventual acceptance of the traditionalists. Now the Pentecostal believers are rapidly becoming the largest Protestant bodies in most countries where they are working, and their rate of expansion among the common masses of the world cannot be touched by any traditional method.

Today the charismatic renewal of the Church is spreading among both Protestant and Catholic churches like a wind-blown fire. Where once men tried to control its flames in carefully watched bonfires, it now has spread out into the woods where no man or church can stop it. Occurrences of speaking with other tongues are springing up everywhere, and with this phenomenon has come an increased zeal for world evangelization. Apostolic Christianity is rising again in a spectacular resurrection of first-century life.

Both at Jerusalem and at Ephesus the Christian community began with an outpouring of the Holy Spirit. The happenings of the Day of Pentecost were to characterize the Church of all ages, but the life of the apostolic Church was lost in the decline of the Roman empire and the rise of medieval superstition and religion by decree. The Church was intended to be Pentecostal in nature from the very beginning, and it ceased to be so only when it cooled its fervor and lost its driving evangelistic force. Today only a Holy Spirit-anointed ministry in a context of apostolic doctrine, practice, religious experience, and priorities can face realistically the challenge of world evangelization.

We will define Pentecostalism as that theological position that calls for all the doctrines, the religious experiences, the fundamental practices, and the basic priorities of the apostolic Church. It is no coincidence that Pentecostal theology has predominated during the two periods of the most rapid church growth in history. The whole evangelical church must purge itself of its complicating vestiges of medieval and Reformational religion and return wholeheartedly to the purity and the simplicity of purpose of apostolic Christianity, or else forever give up any hope of total world evangelization.

It is only this kind of Christianity that is growing at any realistic rate in the world. In Brazil, for example, at least one out of every 35 people is a Pentecostal Christian, and there apparently are no cities or towns without a church. Evangelistic campaigns held in stadiums or large auditoriums attract crowds of 50,000 to 75,000 people, with as many as 12,000 people expressing their desire to accept Jesus Christ in a single week of meetings. Elsewhere, this approach to original Christianity is seeing steady growth, tripling the number of Pentecostal believers in the past decade. Every new convert is introduced to the same set of Christian standards that prevailed at Ephesus, resulting in an immediate witness for Christ. Every convert is expected to witness to his own family and friends as soon as possible after he accepts Christ, and he is to join with other inspired believers in devoted, militant evangelism. He participates in a simple, informal approach to worship that is easily explained to those in attendance and easily directed by people with only little training. The combination of apostolic standards with simplicity of methods results in a winning combination that could conceivably carry out the Great Commission.

The New Testament made no attempt to explain the phenomenon of speaking with other tongues, but only described some of its occurences. Many volumes have been written on the subject, but none has successfully explained it. Like drinking water and trying to explain the taste of the common liquid, it must be experienced to be understood; for it is not part of the intellectual life of the believer. Rather, it is a subjective experience in which the believer pours forth an indescribable flow of praise and adoration to God, going beyond the limitations of his own mentality and language to surrender his vocal organs to the utterance of a language he has never learned. Any rational consideration must conclude that it is impossible, for it is not in the nature of human speech for any man to be able to speak a language if there has been no previous conditioning in his brain. Therein lies the miracle of speaking with other tongues. It has to be either a divine miracle or some kind of hysteria, the choice depending on whether or not the tongues actually are real languages that the speaker has never heard or learned.

On the Day of Pentecost, when thousands of people heard the 120 Christians speak in other tongues than their own learned Aramaic and Greek, there were people present from all over the Diaspora and beyond who each "heard them speak in his own language. And they were all amazed and marvelled, saying one to another, Behold, are not all these which speak Galileans? And how hear we every man in our own tongue, wherein we were born? Parthians, and Medes, and Elamites, and the dwellers in Mesopotamia, and in Judea, and Cappadocia, in Pontus, and

Asia, Phrygia, and Pamphylia, in Egypt, and in the parts of Libya about Cyrene, and strangers of Rome, Jews and proselytes, Cretes and Arabians, we do hear them speak in our tongues the wonderful works of God" (Acts 2:6-11).

In most instances there is no one present who can identify a language when it is spoken in prayer, but there have been many thousands of reports to verify that tongues-speaking is indeed language-speaking. The content of such speech is generally praise to God, often in beautiful prose of the highest linguistic quality.

Today this apostolic form of Christianity is no longer a mere denominational position, for it pervades the Christian community from storefront missions to boulevard churches to secluded monasteries. It has created difficult problems for some who are not yet ready to break with the traditional past and return to first-century Christianity, but it is here to stay. The new Spirit-filled believers must not thwart the primary purpose of the Holy Spirit by retreating into egocentric prayer cells or by claiming some kind of spiritual superiority. The baptism in the Holy Spirit does not lead to a revival of Christian mysticism, but to an active, outgoing, militantly evangelistic witness. Jesus said that this power would result in a witness "unto the uttermost part of the earth" (Acts 1:8).

The apostle Paul never knew any other kind of Christian development. He sometimes had to regulate the tongues-speaking for the public services of the Church, but he admitted, "I speak with tongues more than ye all" (I Corinthians 14:18). He knew that his nucleus of believers at Ephesus would have to experience this divine miracle before his new converts could become the driving evangelists he would need for the Asian campaign.

Paul was able to form a nucleus of believers quite quickly at Ephesus because of the excellent preparatory work of Aquila and Priscilla. It often takes a couple of years to develop the sort of nucleus that will make a movement grow. Missionaries often start in a new area by holding meetings in a private home, renting a storefront type of building, or even holding open-air street meetings. Once there are groups of believers in the area, active teams can be organized to accelerate the progress. The thing to remember is that the beginning group must be in miniature what the whole church is to be when it has grown. No important factor should be postponed just because the group is small. For example, in a number of countries the missionaries did not teach biblical tithing because of the poverty of the people. Now with thousands of believers in these countries we are still having to spend American dollars on programs that should rightfully be covered by the national church. In another case, missionaries were lenient in dealing with some early marital problems because of the difficult social situation in that country. Today the missionaries are constantly losing pastors because of their extramarital problems. It cannot be stressed too strongly how important are the factors planted in that first beginning nucleus.

There are still many places where apostolic Christianity has not yet begun. In these areas the missionaries will need to establish beginning nuclei of believers and go through the whole process of mission-field development. In other places the churches are already far into their progress without the patterns of first-century missions. In such cases, the missionaries should first of all investigate their own religious life and seek for a personal return to apostolic standards. This they can do by gathering together for Bible study and prayer and simply re-examining themselves in the light of the New Testament. There are many books on the subject, but most people will do best to read the New Testament again and ask the Lord for a revival of the kind of Christianity found in its sacred pages. As the believers at Ephesus were aided by the laying on of hands, so those seeking the return to apostolic standards and experience may be helped by the prayers of Spirit-filled ministers.

Once the missionaries themselves have returned to first-century Christianity, both in experience and in other concepts, they will very naturally begin to witness to others, for it is in the nature of the Spirit-filled life to do so. Next, they may repeat the process of prayer and Bible study with the national ministers who express an interest in such a return to apostolic Christianity. It will take a tremendous amount of teaching to change the courses of churches long accustomed to other traditional lines of thought and experience; but for the sake of world evangelization these changes must come. Jesus Christ founded only one kind of Christianity, and that was the one taught and experienced by His apostles in the first century. No other historical form of the Church will ever be able to evangelize the world.

In summary, the masses of men do not think in logical patterns. Therefore, the world evangelist must form a nucleus of properly oriented believers who can later become the prototypes for the masses to follow. Such a nucleus must represent apostolic Christianity in all possible ways if the resulting church is to be evangelistic in the New Testament sense.

5. The Role of Mass Communications

PRINCIPLE: *To evangelize large numbers of people, the missionary must somehow bring his message to the attention of the public and break down the masses into workable groups of favorable individual contacts.*

As we consider the missionary methods of the apostle Paul at Ephesus, we must bear in mind the widespread goal that he had envisioned for his Asian center. Paul had chosen his location because it was the vital heart of communications and commerce for a vast region, covering the Province of Asia and reaching out almost indefinitely along the major trade routes and shipping lines. It was essential to his planned objective that he would have to bring the gospel to the attention of a large number of people so that the Christian faith would spread spontaneously with the movement of the people.

Once Paul had established his nucleus of representative believers with whom the new converts could identify, he moved from his private meetings into the next phase of the development of his Ephesian campaign—the mass communication of his message.

As we have observed, Paul had made a preliminary contact with the Ephesian Jewish community on his previous visit two years earlier. In the spring of A.D. 52 he "entered into the synagogue, and reasoned with the Jews. When they desired him to tarry longer time with them, he consented not; but bade them farewell, saying, I must by all means keep this feast that cometh in Jerusalem: but I will return again unto you, if God will. And he sailed from Ephesus" (Acts 18:19-21). Two years later, Paul took advantage of this opportunity, for he "went into the synagogue, and spake boldly for the space of three months, disputing and persuading the things concerning the kingdom of God" (Acts 19:8).

The Jewish influence in Asia was so spread over the area, and the contemporary mentality of the Asian Jews was so weakened by Hellenism, that this format of mass communications allowed Paul and his team to get the message of the Way all over the province in a relatively short period of time. Paul continued to proclaim the gospel in the synagogue until his message became such a public issue that it was no longer possible to gain from that particular method, for "when divers were hardened, and believed not, but spake evil of that way before the multitude, he departed from them and separated the disciples" (Acts 19:9).

The whole point of Paul's mass evangelization was to separate from the masses those people who were willing to accept Jesus Christ, and then to lead those new disciples into a full Christian experience and maturity. Without the goal of separating disciples, his mass evangelism would have been only a spectacular game, something like making love with no intention of bearing children. Irresponsible mass evangelism at Ephesus could have ruined the chances of establishing lasting churches in Asia.

Paul's particular method of mass evangelization was successful because of the rather loose structure of the synagogues. Their openness to the lay participation of Jewish men gave Paul a public format for his message, offering him access to large numbers of people in a brief time. An additional factor that gave Paul an advantage in Asia was the nontraditional views of the local Jewish people. They had already demonstrated a predilection for new modes of thought, for they had openly accepted the radical teachings of John the Baptist as proposed by the Alexandrian liberal, Apollos. Thus, the Ephesian synagogue was an open field for Christian evangelization.

Paul used many techniques of mass communications during his long career, yet one pattern of his work stands out clearly. He always attempted to bring his message to the attention of the public so that from the masses he could separate converts and develop lasting churches.

For the gospel to be widely known it must be widely proclaimed. Hence, at some point a successful missionary enterprise must turn to some form of mass evangelization. Large-scale communications are not in themselves sufficient to accomplish the Great Commission, but they can help to prepare the public for acceptance of the gospel and can provide a practical means to break down the masses into workable numbers of favorable contacts and converts. Mass communication of the gospel is absolutely essential to any realistic plan for total world evangelization.

Nevertheless, in spite of the positive examples of group evangelism by Jesus and His apostles, there are still some Christian leaders who frown on mass evangelism as beneath the dignity of the traditional church. Soured by unfortunate experiences and poorly educated in the subject of mass communications by most theology schools, they reject mass evangelism as a method and continue to foster and abide by their time-honored but now ineffective methods of one-to-one witnessing and publicly isolated church services. Personal witnessing and church services with a low public profile will continue, of course; but as sole methods they are no longer practical solutions to the problem of total world evangelization.

Such rejection of public proclamation in the name of religious tradition is a tragic error, for while the churches that hold such limited views grow only by adding a convert at a time, the world's population increases by 195,000 new human beings per day. The serious world evangelist has no alternative but to turn to the mass communication of the gospel, because if Christianity is to form a massive movement of spontaneous lay evangelization, then at some point it must be publicly proclaimed.

Rather than eliminate mass evangelism on the basis of unfavorable experiences, the serious Christian witness needs to examine the purpose of the method and see how it fits into the total evangelistic approach of the Church. Here again one comes to the nature of the masses and how the public is moved to action. Most mass evangelistic failures may be attributed to a lack of proper perspective, a disregard for the conservation of results through the application of good follow-up techniques, or a misunderstanding of the intuitive nature of public mentality.

If the masses are indeed irrational and react only favorably or unfavorably to symbolic images, then it would be folly to approach the general public with any concept that requires anything more than rudimentary responses. We must be careful not to sell the public short, for people are very unpredictable when they get together to form even random groups; but we yet must recognize the peculiarities of social psychology. Mass communication must be considered for what it really is—a particular approach to large numbers of people to produce an affirmative or a negative reaction. As some men respond affirmatively, they can be separated from the masses and directed into a personal, rational, and willful commitment to a cause or a product. Given enough time, resources, and access to the public, any mass communication that develops a controversy is certain to gain a percentage of followers and sympathizers. One needs only to consider the great variety of human group loyalties to know that this concept of mass mentality is true.

In major advertising, for example, there is seldom any serious attempt to define a product or to go into detail about its characteristics. The advertiser wants only one thing—a favorable public mood for acceptance of his product that leads to an increase in sales. He does not try to sell products to the public; he offers symbols. He researches the market for his product to determine the psychological needs of at least a segment of the masses, reduces those needs to symbols, and then publicly associates his product with the symbols he has chosen.

The chemical contents of a carbonated beverage may be listed on the bottle to meet legal regulations, but in public advertising the promoters of a soft drink claim such popularly desired qualities as refreshment, reality, a cleaner environment, or even international understanding. The fact that caffeine is a drug that produces a mild feeling of euphoria never appears in national advertising. Rather, the coffee ads abound with such publicly accepted words as smooth, rich, natural, blend, and companionship. Cigarette ads do not sell nicotine, tars, and emphysema. They offer sophistication, popularity, masculinity, and femininity—although by what alchemy the same product can make women beautiful and men rugged is never defined. The plain fact is that the public is gullible. Masses of men respond intuitively, not rationally. Spend enough money on well-researched psychological advertising, and the public will respond to almost anything. There is always a little cultural drag while a new idea replaces an old one, but given enough time and patience the public can be talked into anything, if the right motivational buttons are pushed.

Nowhere are such methods more obvious than in our political campaigns. Voters have no opportunity to know the real candidates, but must rely on the views expressed through the mass media. Thus, they do not vote for the man but for a symbol produced by the hired image-makers.

The individual thinker cannot help but be critical of the ethics of modern advertising, public relations, and political campaigning. However, he must accept that today's opinion makers—the popular mood evokers—are right about the nature of mass mentality. The problem that group consciousness has been unscrupulously used by some marketers of products and ideas does not change the fact that motivational research has revealed the true character of the symbolic thinking patterns of public man.

Christian mass evangelism differs from other kinds of mass communication only in the nature of the message and its ability to prove its claims through the demonstration of observable answers to prayer. As the drives of mass psychology are subconscious and irrational, the approaches of Christian communications must limit their appeal to a polarization of public opinion rather than attempting to lead the multitudes immediately into a full understanding of doctrine. If the masses think in symbolic images and are moved by the general mood of the majority, then mass evangelism should take advantage of the factors of Christianity that can best appeal to the multitudes. Such image-making can provide convenient cultural pegs upon which the masses may hang their prejudices and around which people may cluster in search of order out of the mass chaos. Although large groups may not think rationally, they are made up of individuals who seek their own personal good and are willing to rally around causes and beliefs that offer them some kind of order out of the random patterns of mass behavior.

The world evangelist must also remember that not all men will submerge into the group consciousness of the masses. Education tends to separate men from mass thinking and gives them the ability to remain aloof from mass behavior. This is only a tendency, though, for only a minor percentage of educated people ever attain the best of what education can give them. Another factor that separates men from the masses is culture. The persons of one cultural group or society will not normally submerge into the mass reactions of a different social group than their own, particularly if they consider the reacting group to be inferior. There is also the factor that every social enclave has its own set of values and symbolic imagery. Mass thinking is very complicated to understand, but the masses can respond with surprising simplicity when the right symbols are presented. A single flag waving in the breeze can evoke infinitely more response in the masses than the most eloquent discourse on patriotism.

This is not to say that the Church must limit itself to the use of the historical Christian symbols. The cross has certainly provided a militant standard for the Church throughout the centuries, and the visible symbols of the eucharistic bread and wine have established a popular identification with deity. Public baptism is a ceremonial act that symbolically buries a man's sinful past and resurrects him to a new life in Christ. These are excellent examples of the adaptation of Christianity to the image-thinking of the masses, but they are only samples of the great field of image-making and mood evocation available to the Church. Another way to say that the public thinks in images is to say that the masses think in analogies. Jesus constantly supplied the masses with parables that took the simple things of the group culture and gave them new meaning by illustrating eternal truths. The parables not only provided a mass context for Jesus' message, but placed memory tags on the daily activities and objects of life that constantly reminded the common people of His divine teachings.

Mass evangelists must learn well their lesson in analogous presentation. The public will not be moved by theological discourses on the efficacy of prayer, but it will respond warmly and abundantly to the personal testimony of a man whose prayers were demonstratably answered. A single public example of the healing of a blind man can say infinitely more to the masses than a library of books on divine healing. The old saying that a picture is worth a thousand words precisely pinpoints the problem in public proclamation of any message: to communicate with the masses one must speak in word pictures and provide a visual context in which new thought patterns can be expressed.

Most of the time people take the Church for granted. It is an expected part of the community, and the public goes by outside its hallowed walls with not so much as a glance. The Church fills a cultural niche that society has made for it and where that same society buries it in a conceptual anonymity as a dog buries a bone. Somehow the Church must regain the attention of the public or it will fade entirely from view among the billboards and the gasoline stations.

What Marshall McLuhan said of products can apply to church buildings as well: "A product can become so popular that it saturates the mind of the public and becomes invisible." A packaging-design executive, Walter Margulies of Lippincott & Margulies, also said: "Any product whose package has become overfamiliar may suffer from it; an overfamiliar package can make the product, in effect, disappear." ("Packaging Pressures the Marketing Man," by Robin Nelson, *Marketing/Communications*, October, 1971.)

This is why mass evangelism often is best done outside the traditional church buildings. Somehow the church must come to the attention of the public. When people attend a mass meeting in a stadium, a town hall, or a large tent, they are already conditioned to expect something spectacular and are uniquely susceptible to life-changing decisions. Furthermore, the masses are greatly impressed by their own numbers. A gospel meeting with ten thousand people in attendance has a deep impact on the individuals in the crowd, particularly if the evangelist and his program are able to polarize the attention of the crowd and gain an attitude or mood of acceptance. If all has been done well, such mood evocation will give the evangelist a marvelous opportunity to gain hundreds of conversion decisions. In a small town or village, a crowd of hundreds or even dozens can have the same effect.

When it is well planned and accompanied by other studied methods that lead to the development of lasting congregations, mass evangelism can provide a powerful tool for the Church. In spite of the many egocentric revivalists who go forth in their own name and form their own personality cults, the evangelical churches must not allow the insincerity and irresponsibility of some revivalists and the clumsy abortive efforts of others to destroy mass meetings for those who really do understand the role of mass evangelism and who truly seek to proclaim the gospel and establish lasting, viable congregations of believers.

Irresponsible mass meetings that only play with the emotions of the crowd, while demonstrating no intention of staying to build solid groups of Christian believers, are to be abhorred; for they do nothing to advance the kingdom of God and in fact harden the area for subsequent efforts by serious evangelists. Such religious quackery is like advertising and sales without delivery of the product. If dishonesty in advertising is a crime, then surely irresponsible mass evangelism is a sin against man and the commands of God.

True and effective mass evangelism is often confused with its nonproductive competitors. Cheap advertising gimmicks may gain a brief following, but in the end they only confuse the public by associating religion with materialistic values. Drive-in campaigns that offer trading stamps, giveaway books that offer instant materialistic success in return for faith in God and a generous contribution, sample bottles of water from the pool of Siloam which when troubled will bring instant healing, the sweaty shirt of the evangelist torn up in little pieces and sent on request to bring health and wealth to the sick and the poor—all such gimmickry cheapens the message and brings chaos to any serious theology.

The personality cults that cause men to seek a man rather than the Lord Jesus Christ confuse the public and cause multitudes of searching people to miss out on the fullness of Christian joy that is to found only in the fellowship of the whole Body of Christ. In too many cases, the followers of such men may even miss salvation and heaven. Ego-motivated men of the hour turn out to be as passing as their claims indicate. Like holiday fireworks, they rise in a great splash of color, but soon fade into oblivion as the crowd breathlessly awaits the next display of pyrotechnic artistry.

In the view of many churches, mass evangelism is just busy work. By putting on some big display of effusion to the world, the Church demonstrates its charitable concern for all the poor people who have the misfortune of dwelling outside the church's protective walls, then it can retreat again to its reclusive shell and forget the world for another year. Such minimally motivated efforts are ineffective because the Church really does not want all those outsiders coming in to upset its well-ordered and secure ecclesiastical society.

Even many sincere evangelistic efforts fail because they are viewed as terminal projects rather than as tools for continuous church growth. Someone suggests a revival campaign, and everybody thinks it would be a good idea, so they have their campaign and all cancel their local meetings to attend. When the two weeks of meetings are over, they discover that there are no new converts in any of the cooperating churches and the local attendance of the churches has actually declined because the doors were closed for two weeks. What went wrong? First, the campaign had nothing to do with the development of the local churches. It was a sort of vacation from local church services instead of an increased activity surrounding the churches. Most of the people who attended the campaign were from churches of the area, so even if they gave the impression of converting by responding in some way they returned to their own churches after the campaign was over. Second, the campaign was not part of a larger evangelistic plan of action for the churches, but a terminal project that produced few results. It was an isolated activity that only brought problems to the cooperating churches.

The problem is that the person who attends a mass evangelistic meeting may not know the difference between the real and the make-believe. There is little difference between the firing of a blank cartridge and that of a real bullet, except for the results. So, too, mass evangelism must be appraised by its results, not by the emotionally charged event itself. Armies do not fire cannons just to hear the roar, see the smoke, and smell the gunpowder; spectacular as a cannon firing may be, the greater spectacle is what happens when the shell strikes its predetermined target.

The right kind of mass evangelism is part of a total plan of the church to get the attention of the public and to break down the masses into workable groups of favorable prospective believers. It may involve the ministries of many people, including those of remarkable individual personalities, but the central purpose will always be the proper advancement of the kingdom of God through the fulfillment of the Great Commission. Spectacular methods may be used to attract the attention of the masses, but they will be ethically sound and characterized by Christian truth and honesty. It may take advantage of modern techniques, facilities, and media, but it will rely on the original appeal of apostolic Christianity for its main thrust.

The format of a mass evangelistic program may vary greatly according to the need, the opportunities, and the culture of the location. Evangelistic campaigns in stadiums, tents, or auditoriums are very popular, but they are by no means the only possibilities. Campaigns held in local churches have difficulty in attracting the attention of the community, but they are effective if programed well and publicized in the area. Local-church campaigns are often helpful as preparatory events to a citywide or regional crusade. Some very good results have been recorded from campaigns in which the evangelist or members of the team have stayed for a few weeks after the primary crusade to hold converts' meetings in each of the cooperating churches. The mass meetings need to go beyond the local church to provide a contact with the community that the congregations normally cannot attain alone. If a planned follow-up technique is put into operation, such meetings can be extremely successful for bringing in new converts.

Campaign evangelism is not the only way to reach the masses. The only limitation is the creative imagination of the Church and its willingness to exploit the many possibilities available today. Few missions planners would have predicted a gospel television ministry out of Ouagadougou, Upper Volta, or an entrance to Calcutta through a program of judo instruction. Yet missionaries are successfully bringing their message to the attention of the public through these methods. Mass evangelism may be defined as any method or program that brings the gospel to the attention of the public.

The key to successful mass evangelism is for the world evangelist constantly to seek points of contact with the community. Most churches and church activities may be divided into three responses to the world that may be generally characterized as regressive, integrated, and aggressive. The regressive church rejects society and hides itself securely within its circle of piety. It has little contact with the community, and indeed does not desire to communicate with a society it considers evil and to be shunned. Such a church has a negative presence in the world.

The integrated church fits into a special social niche that society has prepared for it. The community thinks that the church is all right in its place, and the church responds by dutifully remaining in its secure position of acceptance. In its comfortable, socially acceptable condition, it is a part of the community without disrupting anything or applying any critical guilt pressure on the rest of the balanced society. It surrenders to the view that religion is an important but not all-inclusive part of life. Such a church has only a token presence in the world.

The aggressive church confronts society with the claims of Jesus Christ and seeks to change the community to the Christian ethical standards and bring its individuals to personal salvation. With its thriving life and its optimistic attack on the world, aggressive Christianity continuously seeks to increase its points of contact with the community with the sole purpose of making lasting conversions and uniting believers in congregations. It seeks to pervade and convert society through militant evangelism. Such a church sets as its goal the total evangelization of the community and the world.

The apostolic church has to be aggressive if it is to identify itself with the original cause of the Church of the first century. There are those who argue that worship of God and fellowship of believers are as important as evangelization, but there can be no such division of the Body of Christ. Modern definitions of the Church and its functions have been learned more from corporate organizational patterns than from the New

Testament. The Gestaltist idea that a thing is more than the sum of its parts is appropriately applicable to the aggressive kind of New Testament Christianity. Praise to God cannot be separated from obedience to His commandments, and fellowship of believers cannot be divided from the loving and insatiable quest for an ever-expanding number of converts. Evangelism cannot be segregated from worship and fellowship, for God is best worshiped by offering to Him a growing body of fellowshiping, praising believers. The Church enjoys its greatest fulfillment on earth when it rejoices over the salvation of the lost. What the Church is, how its members relate to one another, and what its task is must all be integrated into a single, powerful unity if it is truly to accomplish its essential objective.

Mass evangelism is only one of the methods of the Church. It should be considered a very important function, for it represents an expanding number of points of contact with the community. An evangelistic church may be compared to a predacious spider whose expansive web reaches out in all directions to increase the outreach of the hunter and multiply its opportunities for bringing in the random insects that are caught in its widespread web. The local church must be just as organized and just as efficient a hunter as the spider.

I saw a beautiful example of mass evangelism in a united campaign in Santo Domingo, the Dominican Republic. The participating churches prepared for this campaign for over a year to set up the strategy for the publicity, the meetings themselves, and an effective follow-up procedure. Missionaries and national ministers organized well to care for all the details of the crusade. Various choirs prepared excellent music. Youth teams sorted their literature into convenient packets and practiced their techniques for house-to-house visitation.

Just before the campaign, workers placed promotional posters all over the city and hung large banners across the main streets. Youth teams actively distributed literature and witnessed in the residential areas. Special programs on radio and television attracted the attention of the masses. A person living in Santo Domingo could not turn on his radio or television set, open a newspaper, or even walk down the street without being confronted by the precrusade promotional campaign.

By the time the crusade began in Quisqueya Stadium, the evangelical churches in Santo Domingo had already reaped a good harvest of favorable publicity. The most important impact came from the crusade itself when thousands of people crowded into the baseball stadium night after night. The Dominican throng reached an unusual degree of feeling, for nothing brings out the best in singers and preachers like a large crowd of excited people. At the invitation for salvation, hundreds of seekers marched forward to accept Christ as their personal Savior and to have their names and addresses recorded for the organized follow-up program.

One of the main attractions of such a meeting is the crowd itself. The same program put on in a local church would not attract more than a few outsiders. More than 75 percent of those who attended the meetings in the Quisqueya Stadium were people who had never been in a Protestant service before. In fact, the crowd in the stadium was larger than the entire evangelical population of the city. The reason for this phenomenon was fairly simple to understand. The large amount of precampaign publicity made the campaign a public event. The fact that such a large demonstration of evangelical strength became a controversial issue in the community was a major factor in producing the crowd. Furthermore, having the meetings in a location normally associated with spectacular events helped to create the public mood for producing a crowd.

Once the individual person chose to attend a meeting to observe the evangelicals from the anonymity of the crowd, he crossed the parking lot in semidarkness and passed through a dimly lighted entrance through tunnellike passageways to the stadium stands. Suddenly he came out of the darkness and into the brightly lighted, colorful stadium with its mass excitement. Everywhere there were smiling faces and an intense feeling of expectancy. Nobody in the stands knew what would happen, but they were sure that something would occur. The believers themselves were caught up in a wave of voluntary enthusiasm, for the tables were turned on the usual majority and the Protestant minority was in charge of something big and wonderful. Whether or not the people sitting in the stands were evangelical believers, most who ventured into the stadium found the mass mood irresistible.

The meetings continued for about a week. There was no need for them to last longer. Within a few days the campaign had accomplished even more than the planners had envisioned. The whole community was caught up in a favorable mood for the work of the evangelical churches, the government looked good for its broadmindedness in allowing such freedom of religious expression, and the churches had hundreds of names and addresses of interested prospects who had come forward for salvation. Nothing more should be required of a campaign than this. The rest has to be done in an organized follow-up program over the next year.

The purpose of mass evangelism is to bring the message of the gospel to the attention of the public and to break down the masses into workable groups of favorable individual prospects.

Mass evangelism is not the whole method of the churches; but it is an important tool for expansion. What is accomplished by the method, except for the immediate publicity and mood evocation, depends not on the campaign itself but on the postcampaign follow-up program. This applies to any mass evangelistic method from newspaper advertising to radio and television programs, from house-to-house literature distribution to gospel correspondence courses, and from street meetings to stadium crusades. The purpose of direct witnessing to mass audiences is to separate disciples out of the conglomerate mass of society. Nothing more should be asked of the method than that it provide the churches with a polarized public opinion and a list of new prospective believers. By alternating between mass evangelization and the training and maturation of believers, an evangelical church can grow very rapidly and continuously.

There is no culture in the world where the churches cannot grow by combining mass evangelism with a full program of worship, Christian interaction, a comprehensive training program, and the dedicated involvement of every believer in witnessing to his fellow men. Open campaigns are not always possible—as in the Muslim countries—but there is no place on earth where some kind of mass evangelization cannot occur. In most cases, it can be carried on at different levels at the same time. Radio and correspondence courses can blanket the whole region while the whole body of believers is witnessing daily. Active churches can keep up a steady pressure of outreach programs to remain constantly in the public eye. Television programs aimed at the involvement of the individual viewer can be as effective as any mass evangelistic method, for it attains the miracle of one-to-one communication on a large scale, and it accomplishes this in the viewer's own living room. With such a background of evangelical activism, almost any kind of public preaching campaign will bring abundant positive results.

There can develop in the church a cycle of expansion. If the leaders will develop their skills and vision at a commensurate rate, this context of alternating between mass evangelism and believer maturation could bring about the fulfillment of the Great Commission. It is not so much a circle of activities and development as it is a spiral that steadily widens and at the same time increases its ratio of effort to growth rate. Like a swinging steel ball on the end of a long string, the more string a person lets out the faster and farther the ball will travel in relation to the effort expended at the center of the operation. Even a 10 percent growth per year would increase to amazing parameters once the numbers became significant. A church with 3 million believers this year could have 12.5 million in fifteen years, and in another fifteen years it would have 52.3 million. If only a few evangelical churches would go into this conservative growth pattern of 10 percent per year, they would create a tremendous impact on the world.

To reach a given population, a missionary might have to begin by sponsoring his first mass effort alone. Perhaps he would raise the funds from his supporting friends and put on a stadium crusade with an experienced missionary evangelist, resulting in some 100 favorable contacts. Of these, ten might remain true under less than optimal conditions, for he would have no nucleus with whom the new believer could relate. Perhaps of the ten only one would turn out to be a Christian worker who could lead services. Yet, with this small beginning the missionary establishes his church with the few people and works to train his one helper.

With the assistance of the mission board and some evangelistic funds, he then plans another campaign. This time he once more breaks the mass down into a workable group of contacts. This time he gets 1,000 prospects, which results in 100 new believers and 10 new workers. Now he has a church with 110 believers of whom 11 are workers. After a period of establishing his church and training the workers, he goes into another bigger and much more organized campaign, which this time yields him 2,000 prospects with 200 new believers and 20 more workers. Now there are 310 followers and 31 national ministers. There will come a point at which the number of prospects will not escalate from single campaigns, but the church will diversify its efforts into other productive ministries that will make up for the difference. Other congregations are starting to form, springing up spontaneously from the witnessing of the people. It will not be long before the church will number believers in the thousands and workers in the hundreds. Furthermore, because every new follower represents a whole new complex of relatives and geographical origins, the church will soon grow over a broad territory with astonishing rapidity.

This description is oversimplified, of course, for there are infinite variations to every complex of human activity. There are many things to do, such as organizing the national church and developing a Bible school to train the ministers. Unless the structure and leadership concepts keep pace with the other expansion, the built-in limitations of inadequate organization and leadership will stunt the growth and eventually stop the increase altogether. If the church is not organized well, its efforts will become dissipated; and if it is organized well it runs the risk of falling into the hands of leaders with limited vision and inadequate abilities. The worst enemy is fear—fear of taking chances and fear of losing position in office. For this reason a missionary must remain as a dedicated activist constantly to probe the capabilities of the church to evangelize its society, prod the leaders into constant evangelistic activities, and incite the conditions in which spontaneous movements of lay participation occur.

Not all the believers will come from the mass communication of the gospel, but from personal witnessing and the regular services of the church. These factors of mass evangelism only increase the factors of growth. The secret is to eliminate the negative factors that tend to decelerate the expansion rate. There are those who will argue that growth is never steady, but comes in stages. This has often been the case, but it is not necessarily inevitable. The problem is that the leaders often work in stages because they cannot conceive of more than one level of activity at a time. For the churches in a given interrelated area to grow rapidly past five thousand or more followers, there must be a whole set of kindred programs to carry on all the necessary growth functions at the same time. Thus, instead of growing by progressive or alternating stages, the church should be able to carry on all its needed stages simultaneously.

The implications of such an integrated program of mass communications and accelerated assimilation of converts are clear. If the Bible-believing churches are to carry out the Great Commission in this generation, they must revolutionize their evangelistic and maturational methods. The present rate of growth not only will not evangelize the world, but it will cause the percentage of evangelical believers to decline behind that of an expanding heathen population. The darkness of heathenism will grow as do the lengthening shadows when the sun goes down. Somehow we must bring about Joshua's miracle and cause the sun of evangelical expansion to reverse its course in the contemporary sky.

The apostle Paul had only two reasons for preaching in the synagogue at Ephesus: to make the gospel become a public issue that would polarize the opinions of the community, and to separate disciples from the Asian masses. Without mass evangelism he could never have created the conditions in Asia that produced in that province a great center for early Christianity. To have any possible chance of fulfilling the Great Commission in our lifetime, we must learn from our apostolic prototype and apply to our world the same principles that succeeded so well in the beginning.

6. The Development of Congregations

PRINCIPLE: *Effective mass evangelization always requires that the resulting converts be established in responsible Christian congregations.*

Once the apostle Paul had brought his message to the attention of the community, created a public issue, and broken down the masses into workable groups of favorable prospects, he separated the new disciples from the multitudes and formed them into active congregations of Christian believers. At first they probably met in only one location— possibly in the home of Aquila and Priscilla or in the School of Tyrannus —but they soon branched out to gather in houses all over the city of Ephesus. Before long there were other churches at nearby cities, such as Smyrna, Pergamum, Colossae, Troas, and others.

It is interesting to note that Paul had much to say to the Ephesians about the nature of the Church and its activities. In his Epistle to the Ephesians, he said, "Speaking to yourselves in psalms and hymns and spiritual songs, singing and making melody in your heart to the Lord; giving thanks always for all things unto God and the Father in the name of our Lord Jesus Christ; submitting yourselves one to another in the fear of God" (Ephesians 5:19–21). Apparently the early-Church services were quite informal and inspirational. The Christians offered praise to God and loyalty to one another, and they received the courage and the knowledge to meet the challenge of the surrounding world.

In the same letter to the Ephesians, Paul said, "Christ also loved the church, and gave himself for it; that he might sanctify and cleanse it with the washing of water by the word, that he might present it to himself a glorious church, not having spot, or wrinkle, or any such thing; but that it should be holy and without blemish" (Ephesians 5:25–27).

It is impossible to comprehend the strange mixture of purposeful confrontation with society and of tender care for his churches that characterized the apostle Paul unless one accepts his belief in Jesus Christ as the one true way to God. He did not call this new religion Christianity, as it was to be named in later generations, but referred to it as the *Hodos*—the Way. Jesus had said, "I am the way, the truth, and the life: no man cometh unto the Father, but by me" (John 14:6). Paul believed that salvation through Jesus Christ was the only true way to the only true God, and he unashamedly preached his message to any man of any other religion. Before he ever traveled to Rome, he wrote to the Roman Christians, "I am not ashamed of the gospel of Christ: for it is the power of God unto salvation to every one that believeth; to the Jew first, and also to the Greek" (Romans 1:16). Even though this new religion began among the Jews, it was to be the one way to God for all men of all nations and all cultures. Paul cared for his churches in love and patience; but he confronted society so that he could force public opinion and produce an optimal number of converts from the sincere but mistaken masses. Therefore, he preached "boldly for the space of three months, disputing and persuading the things concerning the kingdom of God. But when divers were hardened, and believed not, but spake evil of that way before the multitude, he departed from them, and separated the disciples" (Acts 19:8—9).

The organization of the first churches was simple, copied almost totally from the Jewish synagogues. After the destruction of the Temple in 587 B.C., the Jewish people in exile in Babylon met in private homes for prayer and the study of the Scriptures. When they were allowed to return to Palestine, the Jews continued to establish houses of worship, or synagogues, wherever their people lived, even though the Jerusalem Temple was rebuilt. In Paul's day, the Temple was still an active center to which the faithful would make their pilgrimages, especially to fulfill certain vows; but the daily focal point of Jewish life was the local synagogue. The synagogue worship was to become more complicated, especially after the last destruction of the Temple in A.D. 70 and the subsequent further dispersion of the Jewish people; but in the A.D. 50s it consisted mostly of prayer and the reading and explanation of the Scriptures. It appears that Paul added more singing than was common in the synagogues, but in all other respects he set up Christian synagogues and called them churches.

The Way was primarily a lay movement, working mostly on an informal basis from house to house. Each city had one pastor, called a presbyter *(presbyteros)*, meaning an elder, or a bishop *(episcopos)*, meaning an overseer. Apparently the terms were used almost interchangeably in the beginning to designate the man in charge of the churches in a given municipality. The synagogues also had presbyters, so there is some indication that only Jewish pastors were called presbyters, and that Gentile pastors may have been called bishops. The only substantiation for this theory is that Paul tended to use the term *presbyteros* early in his missionary career when the Church was more Jewish and the term *episcopos* later when there were more Gentile leaders.

The meetings in the various houses scattered over the city were led by deacons *(diakonos)*, meaning a minister or one who serves others, who were responsible to the elder/bishop. The church services were not in themselves evangelistic, for the meetings were not authorized under the Roman law. They had to be conducted in some secrecy and without gathering large numbers of people in any one house. As long as the Roman officials viewed the Christians as part of Judaism, they enjoyed the Jewish privileges and the immunity from Roman military service, but once they were recognized as a separate religion they immediately became illegal. Evangelism was carried on largely outside the Christian meetings, with every believer an evangelist and every human relationship an evangelistic opportunity. There was a total involvement of all Christians in the Way, for each belonged to a small unit of interresponsible believers who met in a private house.

One of the earliest descriptions of a Christian service comes from Justin Martyr in the middle of the second century. Although it must have been somewhat refined a hundred years after Paul's entrance into

Ephesus, it was still much like the format of the synagogues. In his *First Apology*, Chapter 67, Justin wrote:

And on the day called Sunday, all who live in cities or in the country gather together to one place, and the memoirs of the apostles or the writings of the prophets are read, as long as time permits; then, when the reader has ceased, the president verbally instructs, and exhorts to the imitation of these good things. Then we all rise together and pray, and as we before said, when our prayer is ended, bread and wine and water are brought, and the president in like manner offers prayers and thanksgiving, according to his ability, and the people assent, saying Amen; and there is a distribution to each, and a participation of that over which thanks have been given, and to those who are absent a portion is sent by the deacons. And they who are well to do, and willing, give what each thinks fit; and what is collected is deposited with the president, who succours the orphans and widows, and those who, through sickness or any other cause, are in want, and those who are in bonds, and the strangers sojourning among us, and in a word takes care of all who are in need. But Sunday is the day on which we hold our common assembly.

The similarity of Justin's order of service to that of the synagogues probably indicates that the first church at Ephesus conducted its Sunday services in much the same manner. As in the beginning nucleus, converts were instructed, baptized in water, and led to experience the baptism in the Holy Spirit.

A brick is a brick whether it lies alone or with others of its own kind; but it does not constitute a fireplace until it and others are arranged in a particular order and united by cement. So, too, a lone Christian may be saved from his sins because of his personal request for forgiveness and his commitment to Jesus Christ, but he will not long endure in the faith if he does not join with other Christians in a local congregation to form a biblical Church. The Church of Jesus Christ is not just a conglomerate of all its individual members, any more than a fireplace is just a pile of bricks. The Church is not the Church unless it exists in its entirety, for Jesus said, "For where two or three are gathered together in my name, there am I in the midst of them" (Matthew 18:20). The living Presence of Christ in the community of believers was to begin with two or three, which condition would fully constitute the Church. The mystical Body of Christ is not fragmented into congregations, but is present in its wholeness wherever Christian believers gather together in the name of Jesus Christ. A lone Christian does not make up the Church, any more than a single isolated cell can be said to be a larger multicelled body; but when two or more Christians meet in Jesus' name they become something more than the sum of their individual beings. They become the Church, against which the gates of hell shall not prevail.

Examples can be cited of isolated believers, such as the converted thief on the cross or the Elder John on the Isle of Patmos, but these were never the normal experiences of first- or second-century Christians. The writer of the Epistle to the Hebrews said, "Let us hold fast the profession of our faith without wavering; (for he is faithful that promised;) and let us consider one another to provoke unto love and to good works: not forsaking the assembling of ourselves together, as the manner of some is; but exhorting one another: and so much the more, as ye see the day approaching" (Hebrews 10:23–25).

In the same passage in which Justin Martyr described the Sunday services of the second-century churches, he said, "We always keep together; and for all things wherewith we are supplied, we bless the Maker of all through His Son Jesus Christ, and through the Holy Ghost" (First Apology, Chapter 67).

There is no question about it: early-Church evangelization always was intended to lead to the formation of local congregations of believers. Within what Paul called the "household of faith" (Galatians 6:10) there is the comfort of fellowship with other believers, the nourishment of the exhortation from the Word of God, the divine sacraments of baptism and the eucharist, the blessing of the Holy Spirit, and the dynamic Presence of Jesus Christ in a way never experienced by the solitary believer.

The liberation of the individual personality as an isolated essence is a Western idea not shared by most of the rest of the world and certainly not held by the first Christians. The individual exists and acts within the context of a community and an environment, without whose culture, system of values, and influence he would not be the person he is. No person exists in a vacuum, but is only a factor within a whole continuum of aggregated ingredients that combine to form his personality and provide the contextual significance for his behavior. Although the Bible deals with man as an individual and does not advocate his total submersion into a community consciousness, it does assume his community relationships and approaches him within the context of his society.

True Christianity confronts society and seeks to change it to a full acceptance of the gospel of Jesus Christ. Therefore, Christian converts find themselves alienated from their former community relationships and must transfer themselves into a new community identification if they are to survive the experience. This happens on two levels.

First, they identify themselves with the Body of Christ—that mystical community of the saints of all ages, made up of the dead, the living, and the yet unborn, who are in Christ and will abide eternally with Him. Secondly, they identify themselves with a local congregation of contemporary Christian believers, who in effect become his new earthly community. The latter identification is not so simple as it may appear on the surface, for it begins with a local fellowship of believers and compounds into a worldwide association. Ephesian Christians who met in the house of Aquila and Priscilla were also a part of the whole church in the city, no matter how many houses were added. In addition, they were part of the fellowship of Christian believers in the Province of Asia, the Roman empire, and the whole world.

Modern Christians have the further complexity of orders, denominations, and other social entities with which to identify. A twentieth-century Christian begins to look like a suitcase at the end of a world tour; he has so many tags and labels that it is impossible to tell where he began. Although these identifications may somehow enrich the Church with their differentiations, their very variety is confusing to the new converts. A classical example was the Japanese convert who simply identified himself as a Christian until he came to America to visit the churches who had sent him a missionary, and he discovered to his amazement that he was a Swedish Lutheran. There is great strength in the variety of doctrinal emphases and organizations in the different Bible-based forms of Christianity, for it tends toward a fullness of theological development and keeps the churches from forming dominating monopolies that fall in love with their own structure rather than glorifying God. However, great care should be taken to identify new converts quickly with a local congregation and its affiliations in order to minimize the problem of choosing between so many possible alternatives.

It would help the cause of world evangelization considerably if similar churches would cooperate more closely. Without surrendering their own positions or threatening those of others, they could carry out more joint efforts, especially in mass evangelism, and could combine for a wider range of activities to give the public a show of united force. Most denominational differences are of little relative importance when viewed from the position of eternity. Like flags, they only serve as identifying banners around which their people rally their allegiance. Surely there are many opportunities to fly our flags together for a much more effective impact on the world.

The problems of the multiplicity of church groups must not allow us to minimize the importance of individual identification with the Church of Christ and with a local congregation of believers. Every convert must be brought into a vertical relationship with Jesus Christ and a horizontal relationship with His Church, set in the context of a local congregation where he may worship God and enjoy the benefits of Christian ministry and teaching, the blessings of the sacraments of baptism and the eucharist, and the brotherhood of fellowship with other Christians. Furthermore, he will be able to unite with other believers for the evangelization of his community and the world. Because a lone believer cannot conceivably fulfill the Great Commission, it is biblically unthinkable that a convert would not identify with the Church and a congregation.

Evangelism, then, needs to be totally church-related. Too often it has existed in a void with no attempt to lead converts to a meaningful relationship with a local congregation. Indeed, some evangelists and even some pastors have prided themselves in "just seeking to get souls saved" and not asking anyone to join any church. That is utter nonsense —too often nothing more than a rationalization for their own evangelistic ineffectiveness. One of the major strengths of the early Church was that every Christian was identified with the congregation of a particular city or town, and that he was further responsible to a peer group that met in a private house. Evangelism without establishing converts in viable congregations is irresponsible, like bringing children into the world without claiming any responsibility for their subsequent care and maturation. Such evangelism may be sensational, but if it does not follow through to establish and mature its converts it is unnatural and ultimately of no positive value. We must do more than random witnessing in the world; we must, rather, build the Church by establishing local congregations where Christ is praised and proclaimed regularly in every community on the face of the earth.

The principle of church-related evangelism not only applies to the formation of local congregations of believers in each country, but includes the necessity of developing strong national movements that will inspire the laymen of the world into a massive, spontaneous witness of the gospel. The only hope for evangelizing the world is for the national churches in each country to be set aflame by the Holy Spirit and to incite spontaneous witnessing to spread the gospel over a wide area.

As sincere and as busy as some of the independent mission organizations are, their contributions to the total task must be viewed as supplemental to the work of evangelical denominations, for the efforts of non-church-related ministries can never evangelize the world. There is only one way the Great Commission can be fulfilled, and that is by establishing gospel-preaching congregations in every community on the face of the earth. This will be done only by those groups who are in the business of combining mass evangelism with rapid establishing of churches, an expanding training of ministers, a dynamic development of national churches and their leadership, and the inciting of spontaneous worldwide witnessing. Only the church-related mission boards with their great depth of denominational ministry, theological development, and potential financial support have the capability or the size to offer any real solutions to complete world evangelization. Many of the supplemental mission organizations can offer invaluable assistance if they will so order their programs to give the greatest support to the building of congregations and to maintaining the group loyalties of the believers.

Beginning with his initial activities in a country, a missionary ought to aim at the rapid development of a congregation. He must take considerable time and effort to build the right qualities into that first nucleus, for the pattern first established will continue to characterize the whole organization for many years. There is an inherent problem at this point, for if the church is developed too fast it will be shallow and ineffective; and if it is developed too slowly it will be inactive and even more ineffective. The result is almost the same. The evangelistic motivation of a church should begin from the very first day the group meets for worship, but should be paced in such a way that the properly oriented nucleus remains the dominant conceptual force. As the number of active believers grows, the pace of the evangelistic activities can be increased until a dynamic movement forms to spread the gospel fervently of its own escalating motivation. Once the control group includes several hundred people, there is almost no limit to the potential growth it can attain.

There are many influences that can slow down such development. The most obvious is the problem of governmental regulations that forbid religious proselytizing. Where missionaries and national believers are not allowed to make converts, they obviously must act with caution and seek oblique ways to approach the unconverted. Here the Church must consider the command of Christ to make disciples to take precedence over any human law that forbids seeking conversions to Christianity. The Christian community must obey the laws of each land in which it works, with the exception of those laws that would prevent men from their rightful chance for eternal salvation through Jesus Christ. Any law that limits the Church from fulfilling the actual commands of Jesus Christ must be tested and, if necessary, broken for the sake of the lost men and women living under such an ungodly law. This means that some Christian witnesses will be arrested or even killed, but that is a price that militantly evangelistic Christians have paid since the Church was born. The motivation of the believers must not be to provoke official action, but to establish the gospel in each society and build congregations of disciples. There are many ways that the Church can work in a hostile environment. Radio programs, correspondence courses, and just simply moving about among the people and letting them bring up the subject of religion are some of the possible solutions. The hardest part is to get started in such a country. However, once there is a nucleus of believers, the growth can be more rapid than earlier because the national people can get away with things that the foreigner could never do without detection. Eventually, the government or the local religious majority will begin to persecute the churches and perhaps jail some of the more active witnesses. Once they take that approach, they must either do away with all the believers or face a militant body of Christian evangelists. There is really no way anyone can stop the Church, except possibly to fit it into a socially acceptable mold and deter its drive from evangelistic action to social concern. In other words, the only way to stop it is to absorb it. Opposition will in every case reap increased dedication.

Another even more deadly influence that can slow evangelism is the limited vision of some missionaries. If a leader cannot conceive of the rapid expansion of a congregation, then the church will level off at the limit of his competence. Unfortunately, the men who have the vision to begin a project are often not the ones who have the concepts to carry their own work on to greatness. Many of the missionaries who pioneered churches in the bush areas of the world are incapable of operating at today's level of national church movements. Somehow the courage to ride dugout canoes up the infested jungle rivers never was transferred to the foolhardiness required to manipulate automobiles in the thronging traffic of today's burgeoning cities. The work today has not eradicated the need for pioneering bush missionaries, but it has called for a variety of missionaries with different ministries and gifts.

Yet another limiting influence is the tendency to work in cycles rather than maintaining a steady evangelistic program of church establishing. Usually a church will grow, then slow down to reorganize and assimilate the new converts. Then it will grow again, followed by another period of inner development. This is normal and to be desired, if there is an overall plan of action that keeps the church on course. The natural tendency, however, is to leave longer and longer gaps between the evangelistic periods until the proclamation of the gospel to the lost becomes only a token effort. This is very dangerous, for the church must either grow or decay. Edward Gibbon said, "All that is human must retrograde if it does not advance."

One answer to this problem is to try to get the various churches of the area to work on different cycles so that while one is regrouping for its next engagement with the community, another is in the full heat of battle. Once the local church is large enough to carry on its ministries at many different levels, it can apply continuous evangelistic pressure on the public, while still going through its normal cycles of bringing in new members and restructuring the church groups to accommodate them. As there are more and more churches in a country, the national church will go through similar cycles; but the solution is the same as for a local assembly. The leaders should recognize the patterns of growth and take advantage of them so the movement in their country will grow in numbers and in maturity at the same time.

Most local churches and national church organizations wait much too long before they develop a good Christian education program. Pastors usually add a janitor, a secretary, a music director, and a youth minister before they ever consider an associate pastor with the portfolio of Christian education. The reason for this appears to be related to the Sunday school. When the concept of Sunday school first developed, it was a dynamic program of Christian training for the whole congregation and contributed even to the evangelistic ministry of the church. Today in many churches the Sunday school is a traditional part of its religion and culture, and the people attend more out of a sense of duty than for a learning experience. Basic to the problem is the low intellectual profile of most Sunday-school teaching; in spite of the abundance of teaching materials available today, most Sunday-school classes are incredibly dull and ill-prepared—often nothing more than a running discourse on whatever has been on the mind of the teacher during the previous week.

Pastors with the right concepts of Christian education could salvage the Sunday school and make it a powerful tool of their churches to teach their people and to motivate them to the highest goals of the Christian life. However, this is not apt to happen soon because most theological schools offer only a minimum of training in practical teaching methods at the congregational level. The available courses are mostly years behind the trends in the educational field and are largely taken by potential pastors' wives, most of whom will never become active Sunday-school leaders.

There is some indication that the traditional Sunday school is dead and that in its place is emerging a homogenous concept of Christian education that will pervade the whole life of the church rather than limiting it to an hour on Sunday morning.

This homogenous approach to Christian education calls for some radical changes in the instructional program of the local church. The education of the children will be based on doctrinal development and its application to the Christian life, rather than mere acquaintance with Bible stories. This will not diminish the Bible knowledge of the children or the adults, for the method calls for an orderly program of Bible reading in the homes, in the classrooms, and from the pulpit. The Bible is not being read sufficiently to influence lives as it ought, so the Bible must be read publicly and its complete reading encouraged in the homes.

The education of the young people and adults will follow the lines of elective courses, with some courses required for church school credit. These adult classes will not be divided by age, sex, or marital status, but by the interests and needs of the congregation. The whole church becomes a school with teachers mastering certain materials and repeating their courses with different class groups. Courses would include the Bible and its many books, doctrine, and a wide range of subjects related to Christian living and obedience to the commands of Christ. Teachers will not change their curricula every quarter to remain with their classes, but will work with a limited number of subjects, or perhaps even one subject, and learn to lead their students deeper into the study of the Christian life and its related fields of knowledge. Some of the classes might still be held on Sunday morning, but there would be many others offered all through the week. A class might take place on Tuesday night, and the student would attend it as if it were a night course offered in a university. Tests would be given at the conclusion of the courses, and certificates given for their successful completion. This eventually would provide the church with excellently trained teachers for the expanding educational program.

Visitors on Sunday morning could attend classes with their friends, or they could be directed to a special class of Christian orientation. This class could be a required prebaptismal course and an introduction to the church's basic doctrinal and ethical positions.

Furthermore, there will be a plan of total religious education that will include all the ministries of the church, so that the classes, the children's and youth activities, the various intrachurch organizations, the long-range plan of the pastor's sermons, and indeed all the life of the congregation will contribute to a homogenous strategy of Christian education.

As long as the cyclical pattern of the congregation or national church is related to assimilating new converts and making the necessary adjustments to maintain future growth, the condition is encouragingly healthy. But, if the cycle is one of periodic activity and depression, the church can become afflicted with a sort of conceptual illness in which it ceases to grow because its stages of discouragement negate whatever gains are produced by its comparatively unrealistic times of euphoria.

If the masses are irrational and must be approached on an intuitive plane, then the whole rational basis of the Church must be taught in the local congregation. Mass evangelism is necessary; but without a firm foundation of Christian education in the church it becomes almost totally ineffective and even harmful. Mass evangelism is a medium of advertising and promotion of the gospel to separate the prospective believers from the general public; the delivery of the product occurs in the local church where the convert is introduced to Jesus Christ, brought into fellowship with the community of believers, and developed into full Christian maturity of knowledge and understanding. For these reasons, the ministry of the local church must be highly rational, leading the believer to full Christian maturity of spirit and intellect, emotions and body. The well-developed Christian must be the very ideal of wholesomeness and happiness, for it is the responsibility of the local church to bring each believer to his own highest good, at the culmination of which is eternal life in Jesus Christ. In other words, the evangelization of the masses is not very meaningful if the local church cannot deliver the goods that were advertised to the public.

No movement maintains a steady momentum of increasing intensity and growth, but has its highs and lows, its patterns of growth and stability. The many factors that produce an environment for church growth are so varied and combine in such unpredictable ways that every church or national movement grows in an irregular fashion. The secret is to carry on the work of the church at so many different levels that not all of them will hit their highs and lows at the same time. Evangelism that is not related to church-establishing dies when a period of slowness of convert-making comes, while established congregations with a homogenous concept of the total task of the Church merely make good use of the time to deepen their hold on the believers they already have and to train them for the next onslaught on the world.

It is very important that a congregation grasp the concept that each local church is the whole Church in microcosm. The Body of Christ is not fragmented, but exists in its divine completeness wherever it is manifested. There is no Church visible and Church invisible as two separate identities. The Church is one essence, and at its head is one Lord Jesus Christ who is the only humanly conceivable manifestation of the one true God. Whatever the differences in personality, organization, and culture between church groups, there is only one Church in the world and in heaven; and that is the Church that loves Jesus Christ as Savior and Lord, that fully recognizes Him as God become Man, and that fully keeps His commandments as expressed in the Gospels and further illuminated and developed in the rest of the New Testament.

Jesus Christ founded one Church, the one described in the Christian writings of the first century. Any deviation from the doctrines, the religious experiences, the basic practices, or the relative priorities of that apostolic pattern is a deterioration of the Church as originally conceived by Jesus Christ and His first followers. That there was room for some differences in the first-century Church cannot be denied, but yet Paul warned, "I marvel that ye are so soon removed from him that called you into the grace of Christ unto another gospel: which is not another; but there be some that trouble you, and would pervert the gospel of Christ. But though we, or an angel from heaven, preach any other gospel unto you than that which we have preached unto you, let him be accursed" (Galatians 1:6–8).

There are many ways to start churches anywhere in the world, ranging from mass evangelistic campaigns to prayer meetings and Bible studies held in private homes. Whatever the method of bringing the gospel to the people and drawing converts from the masses, the natural tendency of Christian believers is to band together in a closely related brotherhood. Like attracts like in almost every field, but the Christian fellowship goes far beyond the mere birds-of-a-feather-flock-together concept. The Church is a Body, and it can reach its highest objectives only in a context of group motivation, action, and life. In a normal setting of church development, believers will unite in congregations, local churches will join in national organizations, and these in turn will form fraternal ties with other like bodies in international fellowships, which also form alliances with all other worldwide groups of like apostolic faith. It is all part of the inherent development of living churches that are truly the Body of Christ. As in the predetermined patterns decreed by the chromosomes in the human genetic process, the ideals of the New Testament Church guide the whole growth and maturation of an apostolically oriented congregation. Without this regulative principle, which admits that the Church is more an organism than an organization, the separate congregations would remain independent of one another and ultimately fail to accomplish the holy task of world evangelization commanded by our Lord.

Evangelism, then, must be related to the building of congregations of Christian believers. The Great Commission will be fulfilled only when every community on earth is pervaded by an apostolic Christian witness and every man, woman, and child has a fair chance to hear the gospel and observe it at work in living congregations of regenerated Christian believers.

7. Training National Leaders

PRINCIPLE: *If church growth is to result from massive lay movements, it is essential that the people of each country be taught to pastor their own churches, lead their own evangelistic programs, and direct their own national organizations.*

Once the apostle Paul had formed the new believers into congregations, he immediately began an educational program to train Christian workers for Asia. According to Luke, Paul began "disputing daily in the school of one Tyrannus. And this continued by the space of two years" (Acts 19:9–10).

If Paul's ministry reached all the people in the Province of Asia, then churches must have developed all through the region. In the beginning he might have held some church services in the School of Tyrannus, but the movement soon outgrew that one location and spread out to private homes throughout the city and the surrounding territory. The *schola* of Tyrannus was definitely a school with a lecture hall, which Paul probably rented for his purposes. He may have worked at his tentmaking trade during the mornings, for he later told the Ephesians, "I have coveted no man's silver, or gold, or apparel. Yea, ye yourselves know, that these hands have ministered unto my necessities, and to them that were with me" (Acts 20:33–34). This gives us a clue of how Paul financed himself and his team. No doubt the local congregations cared for their own expenses with their regular Sunday offerings.

Apparently, Paul would rise before dawn to begin his tentmaking and would continue until the fifth hour—an hour before noon. This was the customary work day in Graeco-Roman times. One of the manuscripts of the Acts adds the interesting information that Paul taught in the

School of Tyrannus from the fifth to the tenth hour—from about eleven A.M. until four P.M.—thus indicating that the facilities that bore the name Tyrannus indeed were used as a school, for no first-century church held its meetings at those hours.

The King James Bible says that Paul was disputing in the school, but a better translation would say he was delivering discourses. The Greek word used was the one from which we get our word "dialogue." These were not church services, but teaching lectures in which Paul defended the Christian faith and trained his future church leaders. It is probable that he gathered about himself a group of Asian disciples whom he employed in his textile business in the mornings and taught in the afternoons. In addition to his more limited group of disciples, Paul also opened his discourses to the public for both Christians and non-Christians. Thus, the school provided him with a method of training his followers and of continuing his program of mass evangelism at the same time. No doubt people came from far and wide to listen to the discourses of this controversial teacher who spoke such radical religious ideas, and then they would take the gospel back to their homes all through Asia and along the busy trade routes to the East. He had chosen his center well, and he made certain that it influenced a vast region.

It seems unlikely that Paul used his team to teach in the school, for it was not the style of those times. The school would have been a one-man institution like other such schools of the period. Paul studied under Gamaliel; in like manner the Asian Christians studied under Paul. The most obvious solution to the activities of the rest of the team is that they were busy establishing the churches in Ephesus and throughout the province.

The most impressive result of these two years of missionary ministry is not the pervading Christian witness that was accomplished, but the fact that Paul and his team could continue on to other fields and leave Asia in the hands of the Asians after such a brief period. Some of the members of Paul's team, such as Timothy and Titus, were to have considerable further ministry in Asia, and the apostle John was to spend his last years in Ephesus teaching such men as Ignatius and Polycarp.

The contribution of missionaries was not over, but after only two years the churches were able to carry on their own programs without close foreign supervision.

If the Church is to attain a worldwide lay movement of spontaneous evangelism, it must provide excellent training at three levels. First, such a movement will require a comprehensive program to qualify hundreds of thousands of dedicated lay workers for the task of pervading the world with the Christian witness. Second, it will need a Bible-school program to provide ministerial training for a large number of pastors and evangelists. Third, as leaders emerge from the primary and secondary workers, there will develop a continuing need for advanced theological training to prepare national leaders, teachers, writers, and pastors for the larger and more progressive churches.

The principle of training national believers to carry on the Christian work in their own countries admits that the world will never be evangelized by foreign missionaries. The missionary is a catalyst, an agitator, a mover of men, an inciter of mass movements, who inspires the people of a land to reach their own nation for Christ. In every country where the church requires foreign assistance, the missionary staff should accept as its major task the role of teaching and motivating those who must accomplish the real work of missions.

As long as missionaries remain in control of a national church, the development of the indigenous leadership will be stunted and there will form antiforeign attitudes that will doom the mission to failure. The task of the missionary is to teach the Christian believers of each nation to evangelize their own people and to incite in each country the conditions in which spontaneous lay movements of church expansion will occur. This will require that the evangelical churches be willing to break with their honorable but ultimately ineffective traditions and to move with decisive courage into a more productive approach to world evangelization.

Today's missionary must be professional in every respect. His job is a complicated one that requires a depth of knowledge and experience that always seems to be just beyond him. With little supervision and constantly troubled by the sincere but inept activities of amateurs in his field, he faces the nearly impossible duty of building a national church that will develop into a thriving evangelistic movement. The kind of missionary who starts a church and continues to pastor it and oversee its surrounding territory should become a memory of the past, as a growing number of national ministers take up the role of leading the churches in their own countries.

This is not to say that the number of missionaries will diminish. As the churches increase and grow overseas, they will need the help of more missionaries, not less. This has been the experience of indigenous-minded mission boards wherever national leadership has been allowed to develop and direct its own activities. The new kind of missionary supplements the work of national leaders and provides evangelistic advice and cooperation for local pastors, without permitting himself to become a threat to the emerging leaders. He works in training missions in Bible schools, ministers' institutes, short-term courses in local churches, and with correspondence courses. Others dedicate themselves to holding evangelistic campaigns, or at least assisting with the behind-the-scenes coordination, in cooperation with the national churches. Still others enter specialized ministries in literature, radio and television, and other technical fields. Most successful missionaries travel constantly among the churches, encouraging the pastors, offering assistance wherever they find difficulties, and stimulating the growth of the churches into virgin territory. The missionary who does these tasks well and retains a brotherly relationship with the national believers, while avoiding becoming a threat to national leaders and pastors, will never be out of a job. He will always face a larger task than he can ever accomplish in one lifetime. The idea that the job of a missionary is to work himself out of a job was never true, but there is less reason to believe the myth today than ever before in the history of the Church. There will always be a need for international cooperation, but the roles of foreigners representing Christian organizations in other countries will change as the national churches develop into maturity.

The way to escalate the development of national churches is to provide adequate training for its leaders. Of necessity, the training programs must be based on a practical approach to world evangelization rather than academic methods that seek accreditation and a full, general education. They must be oriented to strong dedication to the cause of Christ, so that students who come out of these training programs will have a practical knowledge of the Bible and an intense motivation to evangelize their own people. This is not to say that higher education should be discouraged or even that the churches should not sponsor academic schools. There will be an increasing need for highly educated Christian believers; but seminaries and other theological schools will never be able to supply the kind or the quantity of graduates needed for the common ministries of the churches in a context of total world witness.

Today's educational process is both a blessing and a curse, presenting the evangelical churches with a difficult dilemma. If a student continues in school throughout the whole program of modern education, he isolates himself from the realities of the human race and renders himself incapable of effective, dynamic evangelism. Having trained himself in the consideration of a wide range of ideas, he often is unable to identify strongly with the basic claims of Jesus Christ with the intensity required to convince the popular masses. Furthermore, he spends so much of his life in the classroom that he leaves himself insufficient time to get the training in language and culture that missionary work demands. National students graduate with a preparation so different from what the work actually needs that they become useless to the Church for its major tasks. As a result, they specialize and limit themselves to secondary roles. Christian leaders must be educated well, but they should be able to receive their training in schools more specifically designed for the tasks they will be asked to perform.

If the world is to be evangelized in this generation, we must offer basic training to a large number of people and elementary Bible school education to the emerging pastors. Higher education should not be required of all ministers, but only those who will engage in such ministries as educational, literary, doctrinal, and administrative leadership.

When missionaries fail to train or to motivate the national believers —generally because they do not trust the national Christians with indigenous leadership or because they do not feel that the people are yet ready for advanced responsibilities—they make the most serious mistakes of their careers. Some missionaries delay their move to relinquish control because they have no clear idea of their own subsequent roles. Others treat the national believers as inferiors whom they privately think will never develop the necessary qualities to replace the work of Western foreigners.

A failure to train national believers for ministry in their own countries results in a limited number of followers and a decidedly foreign church. Many of the overseas churches have ceased to grow because to join them a person has to deny his own national identity. No matter how impressive a missionary's work may seem to his supporting friends and churches in America, the only real missionary success is to teach the national believers to evangelize their own people and to train their most promising young people for leadership in their own country. The effective missionary must honestly operate on the assumption that all kinds of men are basically equal in potential capability and that, given the proper education and motivation, the believers of any nation can evangelize their own cultural groups and cooperate in the whole task of world evangelization. The missionary servant of Jesus Christ must experience his own sort of incarnation; unless he truly becomes one with the people the Lord has called him to reach, he will never be able to bring the message of redemption to them.

One must believe in the Presence and work of the Holy Spirit even to dare approach such a task. The Holy Spirit anoints the ministers of the Lord and inspires them to their best efforts and most eloquent expressions. Some missionaries have the idea that they are going forth in the name of the Lord, but the most accurate statement would be that it is the Lord who is going forth, and for some reason beyond our comprehension He chooses to take some of us along to share in His ultimate victory. The battle and the victory are the Lord's. Beneath the banner of His cross, His legions go forward to wage a holy war, accompanied and led by Christ himself and impassioned by the Holy Spirit to fight to the death for this eternal cause. We may lose an occasional skirmish, but the battle is already won.

This being the case, one would think that education would be a waste of valuable time. To take such a view is to fail to understand the nature of divine inspiration. Whether a man is a lay worker or a professional clergyman, anointed preaching does not flow through him like water through a funnel. The minister is not merely a borrowed set of vocal organs for the utterances of the Holy Spirit. Instead, the Holy Spirit draws on the store of knowledge and experience of the minister to express the divine message of heaven in the thought patterns and the vocabulary of the man. The messenger has to study to improve his knowledge and participate in the mainstream of life in order to broaden his experience and concepts and allow the Holy Spirit to have something from which to draw.

It is impractical, though, to consider a full education for all who will preach the gospel. If apostolic Christianity is to form a massive lay movement of spontaneous witnessing, there will be hundreds of thousands of lay preachers who will proclaim the gospel in the marketplaces, on the street corners, in the parks, in private homes, and wherever they find an opportunity for witnessing. Such men and women cannot all spend months or years in training institutions, nor will there ever be enough Bible schools to offer advanced teaching to the expanding number of lay workers needed. Yet they must receive some degree of Christian education to assure apostolic standards and a continued motivation.

One source of training for lay workers is the Christian-education program of the local church. Every local church should in fact be a school, not only on Sunday morning, but all through the week. Everything the church does should fit into a total pattern of Christian education that somehow advances the participants in their religious experiences and knowledge. Church leaders need to exercise great planning and care that the whole program of the congregation contribute to the learning experience of the members, so that any believer associated with that church may discuss his faith openly and convincingly with anyone who comes in contact with him. The total mobilization of the Church for evangelism cannot occur before there is a more homogenous approach to Christian education that adequately prepares each believer for his encounter with his community.

A new convert should be encouraged to bear witness of his salvation from the moment of his conversion, following which he needs to grow continuously in knowledge and maturity throughout his Christian life. The church can provide both basic training for the whole congregation and specialized education for the emerging group leaders. Each church ought to develop a wide range of evangelistic ministries to involve a broad participation of the congregation, thus increasing its own points of contact with the community and forcing lay workers to rise from the common group. With proper training and direction, specialized teams can be developed to hold open-air meetings, witness from house to house, or organize various kinds of outstations. The breadth of training required for such a program will go far beyond what can be offered during an hour on Sunday morning, for the whole life of the church should be a training medium. The concept of a homogenous program of Christian education could revolutionize the church world and make possible the fulfillment of our task.

A top-level training program in the local church presupposes an excellent pastor with a depth of experience and education. This is a major problem, for most pastors do not qualify for the full training program that their congregations require. There is little use in merely lamenting the fact, because the faster the evangelical churches grow the thinner spread will be their best-trained pastors. If the concept of total evangelization grasps the imagination of the people, the theological schools will be unable to supply the demand for top-rated leaders. Recognizing that the problems of local church leadership threaten to set tragic limitations on the development of congregational training, we must seek ways to supplement the local programs with practical education on a wider scale.

One method of offering outside help to the local-church training ministry is to provide short-term courses on advantageous subjects. Area-wide classes on mass evangelization, teaching methods, Bible and doctrinal topics, person-to-person witnessing, outstation leadership, convert conservation, and other similar themes can greatly strengthen the teaching program of the local churches and make up for some of the weaknesses of the grass-roots leaders. Whole teams of missionaries could dedicate themselves to a lasting ministry of short-term training courses to enhance the work of the local churches.

Another way to supplement the educational programs of the local churches is to develop a comprehensive correspondence school. The whole field of mass education today is facing the same dilemma that challenges foreign missions: there will never be enough traditional college campuses to educate the leaders needed for our modern society, far less provide an adequate base of knowledge for the general public. As the Church must break its stained-glass barrier and get out in the streets if it is to fulfill its Great Commission, so Christian education must stop offering its courses only to those who can attend years of theological training in its ivy-hung seminaries. There is a great potential future in higher Christian education and in the development of better training in the local churches, but these must be supplemented with teaching methods that will supply basic instruction and a feeling of competence to the whole range of active Christian workers, many of whom are neither able nor desire to withdraw from their society to study in the cultural seclusion of an educational institution. The Church can overcome this difficulty and meet the needs of many millions of believers through the development of broadly based home-study methods. Such extensive correspondence schools could begin at the most rudimentary levels and continue through the most advanced college work, thus enhancing the teaching programs at every stage of Christian development.

Correspondence courses are not new. What is new is the growing acceptance of this extension method even by the large universities. This in turn has led to a more honorable position for correspondence studies in the whole field of education. Home-study courses are now commonly used in many teaching situations, but full-scale extension schools are still relatively few. Because of the already structured congregations in thousands of churches all over the world, the evangelical believers provide an excellent opportunity for the development of correspondence methods for Christian worker training. If a correspondence school is to succeed, however, it must resist the temptation to mediocrity and must maintain standards of course development, leadership, and student requirements at least as high as the educational programs it seeks to supplement and in some cases to replace. Properly planned and executed, extension study methods could provide a powerful weapon in the battle for world evangelization.

The Church must constantly remain aware of its own tendency to trust the outcome of its campaigns to the success of single methods. The fulfillment of the Great Commission will require the victorious completion of many programs at every conceivable level of human life. In most cases, the institution of one method should not exclude the successful continuation of another effective one. The existing circle of Christian light in the world is so small, and the ominous darkness of heathen ignorance of Christ is so appalling, that the Church will have to expand its Christian education flame throughout its whole spectrum if it is to see any appreciable conquest of the gloom of Christless night.

The educational programs of the local church, the regional short-term courses, and the comprehensive correspondence schools do not eliminate the need for full schedules of resident institutions for practical and theological training of pastors and other church leaders. If the world can never be evangelized by missionaries, then it must be won by a combination of well-trained national leaders and a massive movement of lay witnesses. This will require Bible-school training to expand the concepts of the ministerial students and to orient them to the major tasks of the Church. Most such schools should accept students with very limited education and train them to a point where they can successfully pastor a strong local church. The minimum entrance requirements may vary from country to country with the levels of educational progress of each local culture. In some cases, underprivileged but highly motivated students can be given an extra year of preparatory courses to bring them up to the progress of the average students. It is more important to teach those in whom the flame of evangelism burns than to seek a high intellectual standard by turning away the poorly educated. The purpose of Bible schools is to provide adequate knowledge, practical experience, and a range of concepts for national ministers to incite and lead an evangelizing, church-establishing, rapidly expanding Christian movement in their own countries.

Even though the entrance requirements of Bible schools should remain low in order to teach the greatest possible number of motivated students, it should also strive for excellence in methods, materials, and manpower. It must use the best of modern techniques available in any given circumstance. Naturally, a school with thirty students learning bush evangelism in a limited linguistic group may not have the equipment or the staff of a school with hundreds of students preparing for ministry in a major international language; yet that does not mean that any Bible school is inferior or unworthy of the application of advanced skills. In the beginning, most mission boards will establish one Bible school in each country, but as the work expands there may be a need to take the Bible school into different linguistic groups and cultural enclaves.

Some Bible schools in metropolitan locations have extended their programs to offer night courses for the believers who cannot become resident students but who are active in the work. This approach especially helps family people who must work during the day. In some places the more mature students in a night Bible school have been more immediately effective than have the younger men and women in the resident school.

The kind of massive lay movements required for world evangelization determines that most Bible schools should aim at a practical program of pastoral preparation, with no attempt to attain any sort of collegiate accreditation. It is inevitable, though, that some schools in education-conscious cultures will eventually develop into Bible colleges, offering theological preparation in a full program of undergraduate and graduate studies. There is really no way to accredit international schools, except by the reputation and excellence of each institution, its faculty, and the accomplishments of its graduates. The goal of advanced theological institutions must not be to attain recognition, but to prepare leaders for dedicated involvement in the evangelization of the human race. Any school that operates only at an idealistic plane with no real correspondence with the educational needs of the students after graduation must ultimately fade into practical insignificance. The current isolationism of many traditional churches may be traced directly to the kind of reclusive educational institutions in which their pastors spent many of their most dynamic and formative years. This problem needs not exist in advanced schools, but it will take a conscious change of attitude and new definition of roles of such institutions to make many of them take an active part in what is really happening in the church world.

At least a part of the problem is that theological schools have a tendency to become surprisingly medieval. Rather than becoming strategic centers of evangelistic concept development and practical training for ministry in the modern world, they revert to Augustinian and Reformational orientations that ignore today's revival of apostolic theology and teach attitudes that despise the popular masses in favor of a sort of Neo-Gnosticism, which limits theological understanding to an enlightened minority. Such schools have been around a long time and will doubtlessly continue to exist within their shroud of mystical traditionalism—thought museums where old and abandoned concepts are displayed and honored for their antiquity—but they will have no meaningful part in the emerging church of the future.

Another problem is that even in progressive schools there is an unfortunate time lag between the latest developments in evangelism and the teaching of such ideas in the classroom. A typical case in point is that missions instructors now teaching in college received their own education twenty or more years ago. Most who were missionaries themselves served at least a decade ago. The concept of the indigenous church taught so strongly over the past quarter century corresponded to a period of nationalization of many previously colonial countries, and it was understandably characterized by the idea of withdrawal of foreign influences. By the turn of the last decade, the Church was ready for an alteration in the indigenous church plan, as it had been expressed by some of its proponents. The revised plan called for the nationalization of indigenous churches, but with the difference that it required the continued presence and ministry of certain kinds of missionaries at the request and under the leadership of the national churches. Time and experience showed that the formation of a national church that is self-governing, self-propagating, and self-supporting is only one step in the contribution of foreign missionaries; but that the divine responsibility of a missionary is to expedite the total evangelization of the country of his calling. A national church needs more than self-sufficiency; it needs to be God-governed, God-propagated, and God-supported—a condition that requires a full allegiance to apostolic standards and a fervent dedication to the total evangelization of the world. The missionary is not working only for the development of a national church, but for a thriving community of Christian believers who will carry out the Great Commission.

As a new internationalism is developing today, it appears that missionaries will add to all of their former work the facilitation of regional, continental, or even worldwide evangelistic and educational activities. There is a sense in which national boundaries have little to do with the Church. Our divine task will be fulfilled only by a fraternal cooperation between all Christian communities, regardless of their nationalities, cultures, languages, or races. The Church is one, whether in Chicago, Mexico City, Tokyo, or Ouagadougou, and its men of God must be considered Christ's witnesses whatever their national origin. If today the availability of American education and affluence puts American missionaries in the majority, yesterday it was England who bore the torch and tomorrow it may be Brazil or Japan. The fact is that God will have His servants to give and to go with no special regard for human geographical boundaries. The very idea of withdrawal of Christian evangelists merely on the basis of their nationality is extraneous to apostolic missionary principles and totally lacking in biblical substantiation.

To carry out the Great Commission, missionaries may even have to bypass certain national churches that fail to become sufficiently evangelistic or that err from the standards of New Testament theology. The missionary is called to reach the world for Jesus Christ, not merely to organize national churches or improve international understanding. Today's missionary still believes very strongly in the indigenous church principle, that the people of each country should evangelize their own people, but he adds to that principle that he is called of God to remain in the mainstream of total world evangelization and continue in meaningful ministry until the greater task is done.

Yet, while such conceptual development is occurring in the field of foreign missions, current missions instructors are teaching the withdrawal of missionary forces whenever a national church becomes self-governing, self-propagating, and self-supporting, regardless of the national church's other characteristics—like growing only to 30,000 believers in a nation of 30 million people. While more missionaries go into foreign service than ever before in history, instructors continue to say that the job of the missionary is to work himself out of a job.

This time lag between concept development and college teaching is not inevitable even though it is overcome only with difficulty. The gap between men who teach and men who do is a major educational problem, which can be bridged only by involving the teachers in the doing process, including the doers in the teaching process, or accomplishing both through an open exchange between the two groups. College mission instructors should be brought into the main flow of mission thinking, perhaps by being oriented along with the missionaries themselves. Even more important, the mission curriculum of a Bible college should be strongly influenced by the people who lead the foreign mission operation in the field. Mission board leaders should at least be advisers to the colleges, and probably should be directly involved in curriculum development and choice of teachers. The reason for this is to assure the missionaries and national church leaders that there is forthcoming a kind of graduate who will dedicate himself to a practical ministry.

When a building is in flames, the people inside do not need a man who can give a discourse on the process of combustion. They need somebody who can yell "Fire!" and then lead them out of danger. That is precisely the urgent need of nearly 4 billion people.

Advanced theological schools can fulfill a necessary role in the total task of the Church if they will properly orient themselves to Christianity's practical mission and make the required adjustments to keep themselves informed at the forward edge of foreign mission thinking. Graduates of such schools will be needed in increasing supply as the mass movement of lay participation expands over the earth, for the somewhat random activities of those whom Jesus called sheep will become dissipated and rendered inconsequential without the structured leadership of those whom Jesus called laborers.

The best of Christian education must become available to those of other lands as it now is for those of the Western countries. One of the finest appeals for the preparation of national ministers was written by Sir Francis Ibiam, Governor at Enugu, Nigeria, in a letter composed in the early 1960s:

There is urgent need today as never before for the people of Africa to have their own God-inspired and forceful but humble Church leaders. Christian witness has more or less failed in many parts of Africa because crude politics, racial considerations and discriminations, commercial greed and other unchristian elements have and have been allowed to colour men's allegiances to Christ and His teachings. This has had the effect of creating much doubt in the minds of our people, making the Gospel of Christ unnecessarily slow, difficult and seriously challenged by non-Christian religions.

I firmly believe that only the avowed and dedicated African Christian with spiritual depth and insight can bring the Good News to his people. It devolves upon the "Older Churches," therefore, to go all out and encourage with their rich heritage in men and money to train suitable Africans of their denominations with a view to making them competent to man key posts of the Church. While the Governments of Africa are straining every effort to produce political man power, the Church Universal should no longer waste precious time in retarding and discouraging those African youths who do look to the way of the Cross. There is no doubt whatsoever that there are millions of staunch and convinced African youths who do look to the way of the Cross. For this reason, our missionaries must discard unchristian pride, and the consideration of self and show us the Light where and whenever the Spirit so desires; and the Spirit of God desires that the people of Africa should acknowledge Christ as Lord of all and that they should build the continent of Africa on Truth and Righteousness. All the other needs of Africa will follow automatically thereafter.

I shall be glad to meet any of your missionaries who are working amongst our people in Nigeria. We deeply appreciate the service of the Church in Nigeria. Nigerians have a great love and respect for missionaries. They are not all good, admittedly, but without their self-sacrifice, without their moral courage and Christian fortitude shown in their lives over the years as they seek earnestly and as they sought with patience and determination to do God's will in this part of His Vineyard, our country could not have reached where we are today—a free and sovereign nation.

The apostle Paul started out two millennia ago to teach the people of the Province of Asia to reach their own land for Christ. He provided a dynamic leadership that continued to influence the Asian church throughout his lifetime, yet he developed his program in such a way that the Asians pastored their own churches, led their own activities, and maintained their own regional integrity. Paul's own team was made up of men and women from many provinces, their selection for the missionary force based on their spiritual gifts rather than their nationality. It is one of the great tragedies of history that the original mission program of the Church was forgotten or ignored for so very long.

As Paul established his Bible school at the School of Tyrannus, so today's world evangelization requires effective training programs to involve a growing number of participants in the holy task of the Church.

8. Maintaining Our Momentum

PRINCIPLE: *The success of world missions is not to be measured against past accomplishments or present gains, but by the realistic progress toward the fulfillment of the Great Commission and the response of the Church to pursue its task with faith and vision.*

The apostle Paul's missionary victory at Ephesus was determined by the total effect of the gospel in the Province of Asia, not by the successful development of any one ministry or program. Paul and his team established the Church of Jesus Christ in Asia, not merely as a token presence in the land but as a pervading Christian witness. The cumulative ministries of Paul, his specialized team of missionaries, and a growing number of Asian gospel workers joined with the active participation of many new Christian believers throughout Asia to spread the message of Christ thoroughly across the populace until "all they that dwelt in Asia heard the word of the Lord Jesus" (Acts 19:10).

The historian Luke was not the only one who held this opinion, for the heathen worshipers of Artemis testified to the same saturation of Asia, saying, "Moreover ye see and hear, that not alone at Ephesus, but almost throughout all Asia, this Paul hath persuaded and turned away much people" (Acts 19:26). A half century later, Gaius Plinius Secundus —the famous Pliny the Younger—wrote to Trajan, the emperor, that there were so many Christians in the Province of Bithynia and Pontus, just north of Asia, that the temples were nigh deserted, the sacred rites had long lapsed, and the food for the sacrificial victims was finding no sale.

The region at the western half of old Asia Minor was to remain a vital heart of Christianity for several centuries. The Asian church was established on the right apostolic principles, so that as it grew in numbers it also maintained its quality and its evangelistic momentum. Luke said, "So mightily grew the word of God and prevailed" (Acts 19:20). The pattern of Christian missions at Ephesus provides an ideal goal for all subsequent evangelization, for what happened in Asia in the first century needs to occur throughout the twentieth-century world.

Paul's missionary ministry at Ephesus was such that his followers could repeat the process over and over at local and regional levels. The method was not original with Paul, for Matthew's summary of the ministry of Jesus displays the same characteristics. Matthew wrote: "And Jesus went about all the cities and villages, teaching in their synagogues, and preaching the gospel of the kingdom, and healing every sickness and every disease among the people. But when he saw the multitudes, he was moved with compassion on them, because they fainted, and were scattered abroad, as sheep having no shepherd. Then saith he unto his disciples, The harvest truly is plenteous, but the labourers are few; pray ye therefore the Lord of the harvest, that he will send forth labourers into his harvest" (Matthew 9:35-38).

Based on this passage, fruitful evangelistic ministry is to be characterized by (1) a pervading Christian witness to all the cities and villages; (2) an active combination of teaching the doctrines and practices of original Christianity (the *didache*), preaching the gospel in an effective proclamation to the world (the *kerygma*), and healing the sick (the *semeia*); (3) a sincere attitude of compassion for the unguided and irrational multitudes; (4) a realistic appraisal of the problem of massive harvest and insufficient gospel workers; and (5) a devoted response to the need of the harvest through specific prayer and the willingness to be sent forth into the fields of evangelistic labor.

In his Epistle to the Ephesians, Paul spoke of his ministry in Asia by saying, "Whereof I was made a minister . . . that I should preach among the Gentiles the unsearchable riches of Christ; and to make all men see what is the fellowship of the mystery, which from the beginning of the world hath been hid in God, who created all things by Jesus Christ" (Ephesians 3:6-8).

It is impossible to know how much of the New Testament Paul ever saw besides the letters he wrote. At least while he was at Ephesus, he had not seen the Gospels of Luke and John, because they were not yet written. It is probable that he had not read the Gospel of Mark, for Mark himself was still in the East and may have been writing his account during that period. It is possible that Matthew's Gospel still existed only in Aramaic and that Mark made an abridged version of it in Greek. The Book of Acts was not yet written, nor were the other non-Pauline epistles, except for the Epistle of James. In the opinion of the author, the whole New Testament of the middle A.D. 50s consisted of scattered copies of the Gospel of Matthew (perhaps still in Aramaic or only recently translated into Greek), the Epistle of James, and Paul's epistles of I and II Thessalonians and I Corinthians. There may have been other epistles, like proto-Corinthians, that have become lost to us.

If this is true, it is very interesting to note how closely Paul followed the pattern of Jesus' ministry as described in the Gospel of Matthew. The breadth of his missionary vision, his compassion for the masses, and his obvious concern for the preparation of workers for a full-scale harvest of the world were much like those same characteristics in the Lord Himself. His ministry of teaching, preaching, and relying on the supporting evidence of answered prayer were taken directly from the evangelistic methods of Jesus. He preached boldly in the synagogue, taught wisely in the School of Tyrannus, and accompanied his spoken discourses with a deep reliance on divine healing and other miracles.

Luke wrote, "And God wrought special miracles by the hands of Paul: so that from his body were brought unto the sick handkerchiefs or aprons, and diseases departed from them, and the evil spirits went out of them" (Acts 19:11-12).

In addition to his spiritual ministry at Ephesus, Paul also assured the continued success of his Asian campaign by providing a practical method of financing the expanding ministries of the church. No matter what the other factors involved, someone had to pay for the expenses to feed, clothe, and house such a team of missionaries, to care for the large amount of travel over the province, to rent the School of Tyrannus, and to finance the growing number of local congregations.

Once more, Luke recorded the facts of history. When Paul came back through Asia a year or so after leaving the province, he gathered the Ephesian elders at Miletus and said, "I have coveted no man's silver, or gold, or apparel. Yea, ye yourselves know, that these hands have ministered unto my necessities, and to them that were with me. I have shewed you all things, how that so labouring ye ought to support the weak, and to remember the words of the Lord Jesus, how he said, It is more blessed to give than to receive" (Acts 20:33-35). Apparently, Paul and some members of his team worked at the textile trade during the normal working hours from dawn until about eleven o'clock in order to finance the work of the missionary group. He taught the local congregations to follow his example and provide for their own expenses and the care of their people. The method was simple: Paul paid the expenses of the mission, and the local churches provided their own funds. Thus, when Paul and his team moved on to other projects, the Asian church suffered no financial trauma.

Paul was able to maintain the momentum of evangelism and church growth in Asia by a combination of success factors that will still work today if world evangelists will apply them in the same practical way that served so effectively at Ephesus.

One of the most difficult problems of world missions is how to maintain momentum over a prolonged period of evangelistic and church-establishing endeavor. Single campaigns of evangelism, a few months of concerted drive for starting or building new churches, or the exclusive development of an isolated program are fairly easy to sustain; but the coordination of related ministries in an inspired pattern of continued expansion and maturation seems always out of reach.

For example, new missionary efforts often grow quite rapidly once they gain more than a hundred followers; but they level off at about 600 believers. After they get more workers prepared and care for some administrative problems, they grow to just under 1,200. They slow down again at 2,500 and again at 5,000. The upper limit for most missionary-directed national churches is about 30,000. National churches go through stages of development related to the missionary staff, too.

When the first group of missionaries begins to slow down from age and sometimes a diminishing personal vision for accomplishment, the national church growth will often decelerate until a new generation of missionaries can attempt to revitalize the ailing church. The tendency of missionaries to maintain themselves in positions that should rightfully be directed by national ministers and the tendency toward loss of evangelistic momentum combine in a deadly matrix to limit church growth to a few thousand believers when it should encompass hundreds of thousands and eventually millions of followers.

The many diseases that stunt church growth cannot all be isolated and their cures prescribed, for as with mental illness every case is different and its diagnosis describable only in broad generalities. However, the world evangelist can look at the successful prototype provided by the apostle Paul and apply the same system in a healthy pattern of missionary progress.

Paul began with the right Christian concept of total world evangelization, never for a moment thinking that the Church would stop growing at any stage until its divine task was completed. He was not satisfied with a token presence of the Church in the world, but labored for a pervading Christian witness that would take the gospel to every man, woman, and child on the face of the earth. Within this inclusive context of world evangelization, he applied specific plans for establishing the gospel in strategic locations from which it would spread spontaneously over the surrounding territory and along the routes of transportation, communication, and social movement. This done, he joined in cooperative teamwork with other missionaries to accomplish feats that none of them could have done individually. He began in an area by forming a representative nucleus of believers who would be in microcosm what the churches throughout the whole area were to become. These original Spirit-filled and doctrinally oriented Christians would become the central core whom the other converts could emulate and with whom they would identify. Paul then took his message to the public in order to break down the masses into workable prospects, and he separated the new converts from the multitudes into viable congregations of believers.

He further strengthened the growing church and multiplied his own efforts by teaching the whole depth of Christian doctrine and practice, and developed potential leaders to direct the local congregations.

✓   Paul held strongly to the concept that evangelization depends on good leadership. Men make church growth happen. One must never underestimate the sovereign power of the Holy Spirit to provide surprising opportunities, yet He opens doors to men whom He inspires to take advantage of the openings and whom He expects to exploit the possibilities for establishing the Christian faith. The Holy Spirit works through men, not just in a vague aura that hovers over a place or a people. The Spirit of God is everywhere, but His message of salvation is decreed to be proclaimed and established among men by men. In his First Epistle to the Corinthians, Paul said, "I will tarry at Ephesus until Pentecost. For a great door and effectual is opened unto me, and there are many adversaries" (I Corinthians 16:8-9).

If men are indeed the servants of God and the vessels of the Holy Spirit, then there can be no real division between what the Holy Spirit opens and what Spirit-filled men cause to happen in the name of the Lord. For the God-chosen world evangelist, even the tiniest crack in an iron gate looms like a chasm of opportunity, and while other lesser men weep over closing doors and declining chances for evangelization, they march forward with banners flying and Spirit swords glistening in the divine sunlight.

Given an open door and an inspired evangelist, the question then becomes one of method. The successful missionary will recognize that he and his colleagues cannot accomplish the task alone, but must train hundreds and eventually thousands of local people to develop the national church to its maximum efficiency and progress. Good missionary administration and a sincere trust in the national Christians and their God-given abilities will lead to inevitable growth.

Missionaries and national ministers alike will find their greatest success in the methods of Jesus and His first-century followers. A balanced combination of teaching, preaching, and miracles still is the most effective ministry of the Church, and it will draw people to it as surely as fire attracts a crowd. The concept that conservatism and a certain stuffy dullness in preaching are required expressions of the seriousness and holiness of Christian worship is a fatal error, responsible for much of the withdrawal of the Church from the arena of active evangelism. The mausoleumlike coldness of formal Christianity, its churches surrounded by appropriate gravestones and even its hymnal pages bearing the obituary birth and death dates of its composers, provide a morose and contemporarily irrelevant setting for any kind of revolutionary proclamation of the gospel. One would think that Jesus Christ is dead and that His worshipers meet only to mourn His untimely parting. Such death-related Christianity not only will not evangelize the world, but currently is not even convincing its own children it has anything meaningful to say to this generation. Nothing but a living, thriving Church with inspired preaching, creative teaching, and unashamed trust in the supernatural can offer any hope for contemporary society or meet the standards demanded by apostolic Christianity.

Of the three facets of apostolic ministry, it is interesting to observe that it is teaching that accomplishes the greatest stability and most long-lasting results. Jesus said, "All power is given unto me in heaven and in earth. Go ye therefore, and *teach* all nations, baptizing them in the name of the Father, and of the Son, and of the Holy Ghost: *teaching* them to observe all things whatsoever I have commanded you: and, lo, I am with you alway, even unto the end of the world" (Matthew 28:18-20).

Two different words are translated "teach" in this Great Commission passage. The first means to make disciples or converts, and the second is the word from which we get our English noun "didactics"—the science or art of instruction or education. In the process of world evangelization, the art of teaching is to guide converts from interested prospects to dedicated disciples, to establish solid Christian doctrine and practice, and to continue in an inspired program of didactic skillfulness to teach all believers to observe the full commandments of Christ. It is only in this setting of apostolic teaching of Christ's original commandments that the lasting Presence of the Lord can be assured.

The world evangelist must return to the teachings of the New Testament Church and identify himself with its doctrines, its experiences, its practices, and its priorities if he is to be truly apostolic in his Christianity and ever fulfill the Great Commission. Whether in a classroom, from the pulpit, writing on paper, speaking on radio or television, or by whatever means he chooses to teach, he is responsible to teach men to become disciples of Jesus Christ and to further educate them concerning all the commandments of the Lord.

Second, the Church is to preach the gospel. Teaching may take on many didactic forms, but preaching is always an oral discourse in which the speaker openly proclaims the Good News of salvation through the death and resurrection of the Lord Jesus Christ. In his role as preacher, the evangelist is a herald announcing an urgent message of impending judgment and of man's one route of escape from the wrath to come. The Greek word for preaching, *kerygma*, came originally from the *keryx*— a trumpet shell from which early Grecians made horns to blow to warn of impending danger or herald some important message. (Those who tire of long sermons sometimes remind preachers that the spiral trumpet shell was also used as an instrument of torture!) Preaching is characterized by a straightforward, urgent style of delivery, often in an oratorical manner that occasionally bursts into the highest forms of human eloquence. It cannot be done by the halfhearted effort of an uninspired and unconcerned man, but is possible only to those who deeply believe in Jesus Christ and His gospel and whose hearts are aflame with the divine imperative to personal salvation. Preaching is an honorable and extremely difficult art; those who do it best know that they must bare their very souls to the world and suffer the anguish of travail until they see men yield to God's call and bow their knees before the Master. Their utterances are inspired by the Holy Spirit, often striking boldly at matters known only to individuals among the listeners. Often, anointed preachers become so deeply engrossed in their delivery that they reach the most beautifully forceful expression possible to man.

Jesus said, if we may refer to the disputed passage in Mark 16, "Go ye into all the world, and preach the gospel to every creature" (Mark

16:15). Whether by that passage or by various others, there is ample evidence that Jesus expected His followers to become inflamed evangelists who would kindle the fires of a massive Christian movement through the fervency of their inspired preaching.

The third factor in apostolic ministry was miracles, especially divine healing. No aspect of apostolic Christianity has been more criticized or less understood than this one, for it requires the suspension of human reason and the acceptance of supernatural intervention in the physical level of life. It requires faith in God for the physically impossible. However, even though rational minds may reject it and some theologians may seek to eliminate it by demythologizing the Scriptures, proven cases of divine healing continue to occur, many of them with positive medical proof. Wherever the Church is growing rapidly, it is still characterized by irrational leaps of faith that trust God for the impossible.

When I was a missionary in Colombia, I was called to pray for a nine-year-old boy who had a large abscess in one lung. He was to undergo surgery on the following Tuesday morning. The family had never been to our church. Their only contact with me was through a neighbor who told the mother that I healed people. When the mother called, I told her that I could not heal but that I had a Friend who could.

After I had gone to the home and talked at some length with the family, I prayed for the boy. At first I prayed in Spanish, but before I was through I told the Lord in English that He really had to heal this boy for the sake of the salvation of this whole family of thirty or more local relatives. Ministers often leave people some qualifying remark to cover them in case nothing happens, but this time on an impulse I told the mother to take the boy to the hospital but insist on one more X-ray before surgery.

That Monday night I waited at the telephone. At about ten o'clock the mother called from the hospital to tell me the abscess had totally disappeared. The doctor also wanted to talk with me because he had two X-rays taken only one week apart, proving conclusively that the boy had been completely healed. As a result of that one case of divine healing, the whole immediate family and a number of relatives were converted.

Most of the time there are no such records. Those who believe in the supernatural intervention of God in the affairs of men take divine healing almost as a matter of course, while those who do not accept the suspension of physical laws tend to relegate even well-proven cases to a special category of the mind where they store the things they do not understand. The fact is that provable cases of divine healing and other miracles happen quite commonly among apostolically minded Christian believers. Whether or not they are accepted by the world, miracles happen all the time in response to the active faith of God's people.

In one of the earliest books of the New Testament, James told the first Christians, "Is any sick among you? let him call for the elders of the church; and let them pray over him, anointing him with oil in the name of the Lord: and the prayer of faith shall save the sick, and the Lord shall raise him up; and if he have committed sins, they shall be forgiven him. Confess your faults one to another, and pray one for another, that ye may be healed. The effectual fervent prayer of a righteous man availeth much" (James 5:14-16).

During Jesus' earthly ministry, He constantly drew the attention of the masses by His acts of divine healing and other miracles. After all, if "All things were made by him" (John 1:3), then it would require no great act to alter a few atoms, restructure a few molecules, or change a few living cells. He did it all the time. He told His Church to do the same. That no one has yet had the mustard-seed faith to move a mountain does not mean that it would not happen if a man just knew how to pray for it and really believe it would move. In the meantime, the mountains stand as monuments to man's failure to capture the essence of Christ's lesson on miracle-working.

When Philip asked Jesus to prove He was the only way to the Father, Jesus replied that He would prove it in three ways. First, He would answer the prayers of the believers, for He said, "And whatsoever ye shall ask in my name, that will I do" (John 14:13). Second, He would send the Holy Spirit, who would dwell within the believers. Third, He would give to His believers the gift of eternal life, saying, ". . . because I live, ye shall live also" (John 14:19).

In this same passage, Jesus promised His Church, "He that believeth on me, the works that I do shall he do also; and greater works than these shall ye do; because I go unto my Father" (John 14:12). There is no question but that Jesus intended that His Church would live at a supernatural plane where the sick would be healed, the dead raised, and many other miracles would occur. The true Christian believes that Spirit is superior to matter; for God, who is Spirit, creates and sustains the material universe. Ultimate reality is Spirit, and matter is a secondary expression of Spirit in an infinitely consistent system. Physical laws are possible only because matter exists in the absolutely consistent mind of God. The light of a distant star travels without variation over a vast number of light-years, never altering its one speed of 186,300 miles per second. God set the speed of light, and He will never change His decision. Science is possible because God is consistent. Yet God has given to His Church the right to request miracles. Backed by all the resources of heaven and earth, God has given His followers a blank check and told them they can have anything they can believe Him for. It is like a special gift offered only to those rare souls who rise above the material chains of earthly existence and grasp the supernatural truth of reality. While some minds reject such an idea as beyond the reach of man, other bolder children stretch forth their hands in faith to their heavenly Father and with unexpected simplicity receive the answers to their prayers.

Whatever the theology of divine healing, the two oral ministries of teaching and preaching have never been capable of producing the impetus necessary to form massive lay movements of Christian witnessing except when the third factor of miracles has been present.

There is no indication in the New Testament that the Lord ever intended that divine healing would replace the work of the human physician, except in separate, individual cases. It appears that the miraculous evidence of God's power over man's most serious physical needs is one way to prove the gospel to men who are not yet ready for deeper spiritual truth. It seems clear in the New Testament that divine healing was for didactic rather than medical purposes. God does not want to upset the whole physical universe at the whims of happy believers, but He will display His power to prove to nonbelievers and the weak of faith that He will listen to His messengers and will confirm their ministries. Jesus healed the sick out of compassion because He could not bear to see those who trust in Him suffer; but he also did His miracles to prove His divinity to the people and to gain credence for His other ministries of preaching and teaching. He made no attempt to heal all the sick, but only those whose healing could somehow advance His total message. If one says that those who really believe in Christ will always be healed of their physical problems, then he must answer why Christ did not heal the thief on the cross whose faith reached out successfully for eternal life.

That Jesus healed and did other miracles to gain belief in Himself is seen clearly in the event when John the Baptist sent two of his disciples to ask if Jesus really was the Christ. The Lord replied, "Go and shew John again those things which ye do hear and see: the blind receive their sight, and the lame walk, the lepers are cleansed, and the deaf hear, the dead are raised up, and the poor have the gospel preached unto them. And blessed is he, whosoever shall not be offended in me" (Matthew 11:4-6).

Miracles, including divine healing, were to prove the gospel to men. They were to be evangelistic in nature, not an easy escape from the problems of life. There is ample evidence in the Scriptures that "tribulation worketh patience" (Romans 5:3), and that often the most godly of men will suffer sickness and various infirmities. Apparently God does not often bypass His own universal laws except to convince men to listen to the preaching and teaching of the gospel, which should give some indication of the relative importance God places on evangelization. Certainly He must sometimes heal because of His mercy, but it appears that in most cases of healing the purpose of the phenomenon is evangelistic—that is, it is intended not so much for the one who is healed as for the one who observes.

There are great blessings whenever someone is healed by divine intervention, but there are also great problems whenever the Church tries to dictate to God when and how He should act. Such an approach to God reduces men's concept of Him to that of a super computer for which proper programing will eventually produce the desired results. It is indeed fortunate for theology that God does not always heal at man's command.

There also are many problems whenever healing is made a spectacle for a sort of mass spirit therapy. The production-line approach to divine healing has brought little glory to God, but considerable fame to men. When the gifts of God are reduced to a popular sideshow, the gullible public is wide open to the manipulation of all sorts of religious confidence men and eccentric quackery. The worst enemy of the true is not so much the untrue as the half true, not so much the lie as the truth pressed to excess.

The working of miracles held too important a place in the ministries of Jesus and His first-century followers for such supernatural events to be the mere exaggeration of the New Testament writers. They do not appear in figurative passages, but in a straight narrative style along with all the other occurrences of those times. That Jesus turned water into wine is part of an otherwise normal wedding story. There is no indication of an allegorical writing form in the story of the raising of Lazarus from the dead. When the lame man was healed outside the Temple, Peter and John were arrested for the disturbance caused by the event. Without accepting the miracles, the greater part of the New Testament story would be incomprehensible. The New Testament writers did not attempt to explain miracles; they just said that they happened. It was an age of great faith when Christian people believed that anything could happen, and it did.

Men still believe in God for miracles. No doubt there are times when the positive influence of faith brings about the healing of people whose main problems are psychological. Such healings are not to be discounted as inconsequential, for the doctors themselves spend much of their time trying to cure these problems. That healing occurs in the mind instead of in some limb or organ is perhaps the greater miracle. There are also continued healings that cannot be attributed to psychological origins.

A man who was burned terribly in a gasoline fire trusted God that his face would not be scarred, even though his worst burns were on his face. When the burns healed in their normal course, his face was restored without a single mark of the fire, although his hands still witness to the seriousness of the burn. There is no way to say what his face might have been like without a miracle, but the man and those who know him will never be convinced of anything but the touch of God.

Goiters have been instantly healed right before the eyes of a congregation. The physically blind have had their sight restored. The lame have walked again. A pastor in Philadelphia had multiple fractures in his legs from a fall from a roof. He had to be carried to the platform of his church, where he would sit to preach. One night he suddenly pointed to the rear of the sanctuary and cried, "Jesus is coming through the door!" He rose to meet the Lord and was instantly healed of all his fractures and their complications. Those who believe in such miracles do not try to explain them except to attribute them to faith in God.

Most Christian believers would agree that God answers prayer, but few have the faith to believe God for specific responses. Miracles can and do happen independently of anyone's opinions about them. The greatest mystery is not that they happen, but that they do not happen more often and more consistently. The writer of the Epistle to the Hebrews said, "Now faith is the substance of things hoped for, the evidence of things not seen" (Hebrews 11:1). The insubstantial substance called faith, like the miracles it believes in and sees come to pass, is beyond human explanation. A man simply reads in the Bible that God has promised to answer prayer, and he makes a specific request in the sincere belief that God hears him and will reply. Whenever it gets much more complicated than that, it usually does not happen. The most important miracle is that man can talk with God at all; the lesser is that God often gives His children what they ask.

There are dangers to living at only a materialistic level where nothing inexplicable happens, but there are also problems if a person rejects the material world in favor of the spiritual. Man is not a dualistic creature with spirit and matter competing for the ascendency; he is a unified being with spirit and matter so inseparably joined that he cannot even distinguish between them. He does not know what spirit is, but then he does not know what matter is either. The fact that man understands so much more of the material universe than he did a few years ago does not diminish the problem that there is still much more that he cannot begin to explain. Whatever he studies, man ultimately must stand in awe before pure energy created and sustained by intelligence far superior to his own. While trusting in the world beyond the physical senses, the Church must also live and act in the material world. It must not slip into some form of mysticism as a substitute for an outgoing Christian witness. With mysticism on the rise, particularly evidenced by the revival of astrology and the occult, many of the traditional churches are turning to faith healing and other charismatic phenomena more out of a search for mystical experience than for a source of proof for the reality of God.

Removed from its biblical evangelistic setting, along with the preaching of the gospel and teaching of the doctrines and practices of the Church, divine healing alone nearly always leads to serious theological problems. In the garden of apostolic evangelism grow three plants of Christian ministry: the proclamation of the gospel, the founding of believers in the faith, and the reliance on the supernatural power of God. Thus, the *kerygma*, the *didache*, and the *semeia* complement one another and ought to be inseparable in the Church's evangelistic ministry to the world. Preaching keeps the Church working in the fields where the cutting edge of evangelism reaches into the grain and gathers it into harvested sheaves. Teaching keeps the Church working in the barns to conserve the results of evangelism and mature its products into heaven's profits. Miracles keep the Church in the sunlight that turns the grain a golden brown and ready for the harvest. The combination of these three apostolic ministries will maintain the momentum of church growth indefinitely.

There was yet another factor that helped the Asian church to maintain its evangelistic momentum. Paul came to Ephesus with a workable plan to pay for the expenses of his campaign. It is said of certain men that they are so heavenly minded that they are no earthly good; but history is filled with examples of heavenly minded men who also were realistically practical, and these men have done the world its greatest good. No matter what the depth of spiritual ministry, the world evangelist must provide practical solutions to his material needs and those of the churches he will establish. Jesus may have turned the water into wine once, but the rest of the time He paid for it. He fed the multitudes on miracle loaves and fishes, but that probably did not happen more than twice. He even paid His taxes with a miracle coin found in the mouth of a fish, but He also worked in a carpentry shop. The Lord may sometimes supply missionary funds from miraculous sources, but most of the time He expects us to work within the monetary systems of this world.

Paul's financial solution at Ephesus was very simple, yet it still is the most practical method of paying the expenses of world evangelization. He worked hard to provide the funds for the costs of his missionary team, and he expected the national church in Asia to be equally motivated to raise its own funds for its own expenses. When at last the School of Tyrannus was closed and Paul moved on to Macedonia, the life of the national church was not disrupted for lack of funds, but continued as it had already learned to do—paying its own way.

No doubt there will always be special projects where the Christians of one part of the world will want to help those of another. All believers in Christ should participate in a worldwide brotherhood in which those who have available money will assist those who have not. When war or famine strike in one region of the earth, the Christians of other places must rise to the occasion in love and understanding to assist their suffering brothers in their time of calamity. When unusual opportunities develop, the Church must consider the whole world its battlefield and apply its depth of resources to the locations of greatest possible victory. The indigenous church principle is necessary to encourage the integrity of each culture, but it should not isolate Christians of different nationalities, nor should it fragment the Church into nationalistic separatism. Our missionaries' philosophies should not deter the Christian believers from becoming one worldwide family, dedicated to one cause and fraternally united in strength. The sponsoring of Bible schools, correspondence schools, evangelistic campaigns, some of the more expensive church construction where necessary, and other such costs could rightfully be considered within the interest span of the whole Christian community.

Although some funds might go from country to country, mostly to support the foreign missionary programs, the normal operational expenses of national and local churches should remain the responsibility of the leaders and members of those churches. If local believers in every congregation are taught the biblical practice of tithing on their income, no matter what their economical condition, then the tithes of ten working people will provide the salary of a pastor at their own cultural level. The pastor in turn will pay a tenth of his income to the national church. With a few more working and tithing people, the congregation can construct its own building, pay its own operational expenses, and develop its own expanding evangelistic program. As it grows, it can support a wider range of local and national projects, including the support of home and foreign missions. There is no need for foreign financial assistance to such a church. Indeed, the application of any regular foreign funds would cause the church damage and stunt its natural growth.

Similarly, the national church should be financed by its own people. The largest single cost in the beginning is the salary of a leader. As time goes on, the movement will need office space and additional staff, an automobile or two, and funds to operate a variety of beneficial programs. If the emphasis is on the quality of leadership rather than on the size of the administrative budget, a national church will not find it difficult to inspire its people to support such a cause.

There are three secrets to raising national funds. First, the people must be taught responsible giving. This means that they must give regularly and in sufficient quantity to assure the progress of their church. They must learn the true maxim of Christ that it is more blessed to give than to receive. Second, the contributions of the people must be put into worthwhile and strategically important projects. Third, all contributions must be completely recorded and accounted for in publicly available reports.

The effective and honest use of God's money will inspire confidence in the donors and cause a cumulative effect of one believer influencing another until the churches will have all the funds they need for their work. The mismanagement of church funds will have just the opposite effect, for when people give their money to God they expect the best in accounting and financial wisdom.

The expenses of the missionary force should be paid by the mission, raised in the missionaries' own country and accountable to the church of that country. As Paul and his team worked to raise their money, so missionaries and their mission boards must give much of their time to gathering sufficient funds to carry on their ministry. In many denominations the missionaries spend a year in deputational ministry to raise cash offerings and monthly support pledges before they go overseas for three- or four-year terms of duty. Then they repeat the process. This method has the advantage of spreading the task of fundraising over a large body of people and increasing the possible flow of money. It also brings the missionary home periodically so that he can maintain his contact and relevancy in two cultures. This is necessary, for the missionary who remains in the foreign environment for too long finally adapts to it to the point that he is no longer effective for producing change in that culture. A missionary must be a revolutionary, a radical, an agitator of men who can incite abrupt alterations in lifestyles and the development of mass movements of people in other cultures. Such men must return periodically to preach about the central task of the Church, both to inspire the involvement of others and to rekindle the flame of evangelism in their own hearts.

Another variation of supporting missionary work is to ask for a percentage of the local church budgets. Although this budgeted method may provide more immediate money than a voluntary system, it has the disadvantage of being impersonal and ultimately limited by the number and the size of the churches. Both methods have been used successfully by major denominations, although the tendency is for the younger and fastest-growing churches to prefer the voluntary system and for the older and more institutional churches to use the budgeted method. The manner of raising missionary funds will vary with different cultures and economic conditions, but as long as the Church maintains its strong commitment to world evangelization it will always find some effective way to support its international ministries.

Missionary funds should pay for missionary costs and certain kinds of foreign projects normally out of reach for the developing national churches. The expenses of national church organizations and their local congregations should be paid by the national believers. Only this apostolic pattern of missionary finance can spread the gospel in an effective and unlimited manner.

Missionaries will never have enough money to carry out all the projects their vision calls for, so they constantly battle the temptation to spend their funds unwisely or to dissipate their available resources on projects of questionable importance. Because of the urgency of world evangelization and the eventual shortage of funds and personnel as the Church expands, luxury items such as the construction of extravagant church buildings or the support of only vaguely religious institutions should be sacrificed in favor of practical projects that make the most utilitarian use of missionary and national church funds.

Congregations may need to go back to meeting in houses as they did in the first century. At least the Church ought not to be confined to the limitations of costly edifices. There was really nothing wrong with the system first instituted by Paul, even though its pattern was very different from today's sanctuary-oriented form of Christianity. The believers met in homes spread all through the community, with only occasional shows of force in larger meetings.

In the beginning, the churches were in the synagogues, but very soon they were forced out into private homes. Throughout the first three centuries the Church constructed no buildings, but spread rapidly from house to house across the Roman empire and beyond. It did not move into the ready-made Roman basilicas until it was made the official state religion and gained religious buildings from its new pagan heritage. So much religious significance became attached to church buildings during the Middle Ages that the buildings themselves became known as churches, whereas previously the term "church" referred to people, not bricks and mortar. The trend toward architectural worship reached its highest pinnacle in the Renaissance cathedrals. Protestantism generally developed along popular lines, but it has had little further to say about its buildings. In most cases, congregations construct buildings that require many years to finance, often demanding the resources of more than one generation. About the time a building is paid for, it is time to go into a new building program with another long-term commitment. Even as expensive as church construction is, yet the greatest problem is not the money; it is the fact that the congregations cannot grow beyond their own walls without pausing in their evangelistic task to construct a new or additional building. By the time the fireplace is built, the fire is gone out. Worse than that, a new generation arises that does not even know there ever was a fire.

Constantine did not liberate the Church when he made it the official state religion of his empire. He imprisoned the Church inside the cold stone walls of a building. Now the whole world can drive by outside the stained-glass barriers of these ornate prisons and never have the slightest idea what is going on inside their hallowed walls. It is little wonder that they are called sanctuaries, for within their protective bulwarks have hidden the reclusive introverts of a millennium and a half of nonproductive Christianity.

The apostolic congregations met in homes in groups of perhaps thirty to fifty people under the direction of a deacon, who in turn was responsible to a bishop who would circulate among his scattered congregations, all of which made up the church at Ephesus or the church at Corinth. The costs were low, the growth was fast and unlimited, and the community of believers was constantly kept in contact with the world and with each other. It was a beautiful system that served the Church remarkably well for three centuries.

It is probably too late to reverse the idea that a Christian congregation must house itself within a single building, but it is not too late to encourage churches to develop outreach programs in their communities in a combination of apostolic and modern methods. The important thing is that there occur a pervading Christian witness in the community. The churches must not yield to the temptation to isolate themselves in cultural enclaves. There can be no more tragic fate for a congregation than that it should surround itself with stone walls and gaze out on the world through its stained-glass windows.

The ideal setting in today's world would be to plan only a few strategically placed buildings in a community that would hold more than five hundred people. These would be mostly to gain status in the community and to provide places for mass gatherings and regional training sessions. There could be a number of smaller churches with sanctuaries to seat perhaps one hundred fifty people, but with their greater emphasis on teaching facilities. Beyond that level the congregations could be scattered in private homes all through the community. The regular services would be held in the houses, special rallies and an active teaching program would occur in the church buildings, and conferences and mass campaigns could be held in the large center. The Church could grow rapidly and without any barrier to its continued expansion, for whenever a group would grow to the limit of one house it could purposely split like biological cell division and occupy two houses, then four, then eight, then sixteen. It would make little difference how close these houses were to one another, for each would usually be filled to capacity and would be fraternally linked to all the other houses in Christian fellowship and love. There would be continuous training courses and mass meetings in the larger buildings to unite the growing movement and maintain the evangelistic momentum around central points of leadership.

The factors that produce church growth and maintain evangelistic momentum are so complicated that no single consideration ever includes them all. Missionaries and national church leaders alike will do well to re-examine the methods of the apostle Paul at Ephesus and apply those same principles to a workable plan for today. If the world is ever to be evangelized, the Church must maintain its missionary motivation over a prolonged period of dedicated Christian witnessing until every man, woman, and child on earth has had a fair chance to know Jesus Christ as his Savior and Lord.

9. Weathering the Storm of Conflict

PRINCIPLE: *When the growing Christian community becomes large enough to be a force in the society, its evangelistic action will provoke a responding counteraction from the major existing religions of the area. This often occurs when the economy and balance of power are most seriously effected.*

With the all-out evangelistic program the apostle Paul was developing at Ephesus, it was inevitable that the Church would eventually come into life-or-death confrontations with the established religions of the province. Paul's firm belief in the Way as an exclusive religion did not diminish the problem that he was guilty of encroachment with a new faith not allowed under the Roman law. For a while he was able to conceal its growth under the protective cover of Jewish immunity to Roman intervention; but once he and his followers were rejected by the synagogue, his teachings were revealed for the illegal religion that Christianity was to be over the next three centuries.

The conflict of the Church with Judaism came in two stages. In the beginning the Jews had enthusiastically endorsed Paul and listened to his discourses in the synagogue; but after three months of his "disputing and persuading the things concerning the kingdom of God," many of the Jews "were hardened, and believed not, but spake evil of that way before the multitude" (Acts 19:8–9). What happened was that the liberal Asian Jews finally realized what Paul was doing to them and were forced to oppose him. Paul knew this would occur, for the Way had to become a public issue before it could grow rapidly and become a popular movement.

The second confrontation came about when a group of traveling Jewish exorcists came to Ephesus and found that the Christian movement was outdoing them at their own craft. They become so impressed by the success of the Church that they also attempted to cast out evil spirits, saying, "We adjure you by Jesus whom Paul preacheth" (Acts 19:13). Luke said that the seven sons of a Jewish leader named Sceva tried to exorcize in this manner. The imitators soon learned that evil is more than a negative influence, a human error, or man failing to do his best. Jesus had taught that evil possesses both mentality and personality, that there is a devil and that there are evil spirits or demons.

When the seven sons of Sceva tried to cast out devils in Jesus' name, the evil spirit answered, "Jesus I know, and Paul I know; but who are ye? And the man in whom the evil spirit was leaped on them, and overcame them, and prevailed against them, so that they fled out of that house naked and wounded" (Acts 19:15–16).

The Jewish community at first accepted Paul, then rejected him. Later, it tried to absorb the Way by showing that the most spectacular things that Paul did were really very Jewish. The result of this attempted syncretism was that this event became publicly known among the Jews and the Greeks, "and fear fell on them all, and the name of the Lord Jesus was magnified. And many that believed came, and confessed, and shewed their deeds. Many of them also which used curious arts brought their books together, and burned them before all men; and they counted the price of them, and found it fifty thousand pieces of silver. So mightily grew the word of God and prevailed" (Acts 19:17–20).

One of the surprising serendipitous events of the Ephesian campaign was that the victory of the Way over the Jewish attempt at syncretism caused more of a stir among the Grecian polytheists than among the more closely related Jewish monotheists. Ephesus was a popular center for animistic fetishes and a certain kind of magical books known throughout the empire as the "Ephesian Writings." Many such texts have been discovered in Egypt. There must have been some Jews among the many people who were convinced and converted on the day of the fetish burning, but the largest response came from the Grecians who practiced curious arts. This public burning of revered and locally profitable occult materials added many new converts to the Church, but it also precipitated the impending conflict with the major religion of the province—the cult of Artemis.

The confrontation with the worshipers of Artemis probably took place during the annual Spring Festival when more than a quarter of a million people would gather for the Pan-Ionian Games held in honor of the fertility goddess. The hive of the Artemis cult would have been at its most active state during the year as masses of people thronged the streets, the large amphitheater on the slope of Mount Pion, the agora, and the huge temple to their goddess. Like a queen bee ruling over a vast area, Artemis reigned in her temple, and the meteorite within her was considered the navel of the earth. In the marketplaces the humbler folk would purchase terra-cotta objects and the wealthier would buy silver shrines to present to Artemis as votive offerings to assure the productivity of their land, their businesses, their cattle, and their wives. It was the high point of the year for the people of Asia.

It is not difficult to imagine the rage that arose in those celebrating Asians when they learned of the public burning of their religious objects. The Grecian craftsmen who manufactured the terra-cotta and silver shrines and the scribes who wrote the magical Ephesian Writings knew that the Way would have to be put down if their thriving commerce were to continue. Certainly the emotional tide of the Pan-Ionian Games would be the time to strike.

It was the silversmiths who began the demonstration. Demetrius the Silversmith aroused his fellow tradesmen by saying, "Sirs, ye know that by this craft we have our wealth" (Acts 19:25). He went on to remind them that this Paul of Tarsus had spread his dangerous ideas all through Asia, teaching the radical doctrine that "they be no gods, which are made with hands" (Acts 19:26). Demetrius waxed even more eloquent as he declared, "So that not only this our craft is in danger to be set at nought; but also that the temple of the great goddess Diana [sic, the Greek text says Artemis] should be despised, and her magnificence should be destroyed, whom all Asia and the world worshippeth" (Acts 19:27).

The silversmiths began to shout, "Great is Artemis of the Ephesians!"

Soon the whole city was in an uproar as more and more people joined the mob and rushed into the amphitheater, which may have held as many as 25,000 people. They captured two of Paul's associates—Gaius and Aristarchus—and marched them by force into the center of the amphitheater.

Paul wanted to go into the theater and defend the Way, but the Christian believers and some of his high-ranking friends among the Roman officials convinced him not to do such a foolish thing. No one knew better than these Romans that the only way to calm a mob is either to meet force with force or else ignore it as unimportant. To honor the demands of the violent crowd by entering the theater and defending the faith would only have enraged the people the more.

A Jew named Alexander tried to quiet the mob, but when the crowd realized he was a Jew they shouted for two hours, "Great is Artemis of the Ephesians!"

Finally, it was the town clerk—the highest Ephesian official—who restored order by an eloquent address in which he said that Artemis was too great to need such defense. He asked what crime the Christians had done to deserve such treatment, pleaded for such matters to be processed by the due course of law, and threatened them with the wrath of their Roman rulers. When at last he gained the release of Gaius and Aristarchus, he dismissed the assembly.

Other things happened at Ephesus that for some reason Luke did not record in his account. Paul wrote from Ephesus in his First Epistle to the Corinthians, "I have fought with beasts at Ephesus" (I Corinthians 15:32). Shortly after leaving Asia, Paul wrote in his Second Epistle to the Corinthians, "For we would not, brethren, have you ignorant of our trouble which came to us in Asia, that we were pressed out of measure, above strength, insomuch that we despaired even of life; but we had the sentence of death in ourselves, that we should not trust in ourselves, but in God which raiseth the dead: who delivered us from so great a death, and doth deliver" (II Corinthians 1:8–10).

For some inexplicable reason, the situation at Ephesus was far more serious than Luke's history would lead us to believe. There can be no other conclusion but that Paul and some of his team were sent into the arena at Ephesus and that they were miraculously delivered. In fact, there is a local tradition at Ephesus about Paul's prison on the Hill of Astyages. It is clear that Paul and his missionary team went through some fearful persecution to plant the cross of Jesus Christ in Asia. It was a calculated risk from the very beginning. Yet Paul would repeat his claims in other places with the same fervor, and eventually would be beheaded at Rome. Having been a driving persecutor himself, Paul knew the cost of religious conviction and that nothing less than his entire devotion to the cause could accomplish the evangelization of his world.

The conflict between Christianity and other religions is inevitable if the Church's ultimate goal is the total evangelization of the world. The religious beliefs of men have centuries and even millennia behind them, and they are not going to disappear without a fierce struggle. As long as the Church maintains a low profile of activities and remains in its socially acceptable niche, it meets with no opposition; but when it breaks out of its traditional mold and begins to grow rapidly by making large numbers of converts among other cultures and religions, the keepers of the endangered religions will fight back. Such a reaction must be expected, even planned for, because leaders of other sets of religious concepts must take defensive action when they see an inspired form of Christianity making significant inroads into their domains. Even professedly passive societies can become furiously violent when the very existence and veracity of their ancient beliefs are threatened.

The prevailing modern view of world culture is that men everywhere should be respected for what they are and left alone to their own religious beliefs. If all roads were to lead to God and all men were ultimately saved, then this would certainly be a commendable approach to life on the planet. But, if Jesus Christ is the only way to God, then the Church is obligated to invade paganism and share its precious knowledge with the rest of the world . . . whether or not the local political and religious leaders wish to allow their people to listen. If we really do hold the key to heaven, then we are morally responsible to replace all other religions with the Christian faith. The pagan world has never taken kindly to this view, especially when the Church has made rapid progress. The world evangelist must know from the outset that he may die for his faith, yet be so dedicated to the cause of Christ that he is willing to take whatever risks are necessary to plant the cross in every community on the face of the earth. This religion began with the shedding of blood, and it has always required a do-or-die devotion of its most devout proponents whenever the Church has made any significant evangelistic advances.

The leaders of an endangered religion do not have many good choices once the Church begins to grow rapidly among their people. They can (1) ignore the new religion and hope it will run its course and decline of its own failure to penetrate the culture; (2) attempt to absorb it into its own system either by showing that its own faith replies favorably to the questions raised by Christianity, or by showing its own similarity to the invading religion; (3) adopt some of the more spectacular characteristics of the Church to impress its own people that it can compete auspiciously with its opponent; or, (4) oppose the new religion by actively teaching against it, seeking legal action to limit its development, or persecute those who adhere to it.

The Church is in greatest danger from the first of these possibilities, for it has never thrived in an atmosphere where it is popularly accepted or publicly ignored. The Muslim world has successfully ignored the Church for centuries and effectively resisted the Christianization of its people. Only recently have sufficient gains been made in Islam to force the pagan religion out of its traditional monolithic mentality. On the other hand, the Church faces serious problems with popular acceptance. In Europe and North America, the Church's positive association with the masses has introduced many nonapostolic traits that continuously dilute Christian dedication and threaten to render the Church ineffective for the central task of world evangelization.

The growing Christian group invading the domains of paganism must take great caution not to dilute the purposes of the faith with a blending of ideas from non-Christian sources. It seems to be true that wherever there is reality there will also develop a counterfeit. The relationship between the two is something like that of a man and his shadow; the shadow is more or less like the man, but it is distorted and lacks the substance of reality. The Church's best reaction to being imitated is to continue to express the truth and not to honor the counterfeit by recognizing it publicly. Only if many people are being led astray should the Church try to correct an imitation. The best argument of the Church is the total impact of what it is and what it does, not some verbal discussion that only serves to polarize further the thinking of the masses on the subject.

The secret of handling the attempts of other religions to copy or to absorb the Church is to maintain equilibrium and hold steady through the problem. Ultimately, such activities will only weaken the position of the defensive group and cause numbers of its people to convert to Christianity.

Many of the heathen influences that can affect the Church are so subtle they are not immediately noticed. Missionaries themselves may adapt so much to the local cultures that they unwittingly allow nonapostolic attitudes and even non-Christian doctrines to develop. In a strongly fatalistic society, the congregations can become too passive for any effective evangelization of their culture. In North America, the prevailing concept of the independent existence of the individual person apart from his relationships to other people has made possible the practice of open communion in which the eucharist is served indiscriminately to anyone sitting in the congregation—a definitely nonapostolic practice. Missionaries must identify with a culture enough to communicate well both orally and by their actions, but they must not adopt the foreign culture to the point where they will not bring about cultural change, incite the growth of an aggressive Christian movement, and keep the Church pure from the defilements of nonapostolic traits.

The Church must always resist the temptation of syncretism, for only the pure Christianity of the New Testament can accomplish the holy task of world evangelization. If Christ is the only Savior, then there can be no compromise with other gods or with nonapostolic concepts. There is no way to unite Buddhism with Christianity without losing the essence of the Church. Even though the cultures of predominantly Buddhist countries may color the personality of the churches in those lands, the basic doctrines, religious experiences, practices, and priorities of apostolic Christianity ought not to be effected. That the Japanese remove their shoes before entering the church does not effect their apostolicity; but the Hindu aversion to blood sacrifices must not cause the churches of India to underemphasize the significance of the sacrificial death and the glorious resurrection of Jesus Christ. Converts from Islam will continue to have a deep sense of community life. Those saved from animism will have a tendency toward an overconcern with evil spirits.

The early Church demonstrated this characteristic to change its emphases subtly with its invasion of different geographical-cultural areas. While it was centered in Judea, it was concerned with the legalistic aspects of the new religion because of these same attitudes in Judaism. When the center moved westward to the Grecian areas, the emphasis changed to a more open system based on the charismatic experiences of the believers—learned not only from Christianity, but from such pilgrimage points as the Oracle of Delphi! When the Church developed even farther westward into Roman territory, it became overly concerned with the structure of religious government—learned from the very masters of public order and governing hierarchies.

The Church must continuously guard itself from the deadly disease of compromise. The Way first established by Jesus and taught us by His apostles must not be diluted with the religious experiments of men, no matter how honorably traditional they may have become. The blending of the Christian faith with the world can do nothing but improve the world, but it will utterly destroy the kind of religion the Church was meant to represent. A little sugar in water will sweeten the liquid and make it a more pleasant drink; but a little water in the sugar will cause it to harden into almost useless lumps. The current blending of faiths and church denominations in the Ecumenical Movement can mostly be summarized by the one word "syncretism." Never has the Church benefited from interfaith dialogue, for Christianity is a militant attack on the many established but mistaken religious beliefs of the world. It is not just an interesting but not exclusive variation on the theme of monotheism. The Way was meant to be the only way. Any dilution of its doctrines, experiences, practices, or priorities with nonapostolic beliefs will weaken its position and ultimately destroy it. The attempts on the life of apostolic Christianity have been many, but each time it dies in one place it rises to new life in another. Fortunately, Jesus said that the gates of hell would not prevail against His Church.

The practice of burning fetishes and other religious objects in a public demonstration is still widely done. It is a powerful way to symbolize the complete break of new converts with the past, and it provides a purifying influence in the churches. Many have been the instances when believers of long standing have come forward at such a burning to repent of hidden sin and offer some revered object held back from their heathen past life. The burning of material symbols of a rejected religion is a dangerous practice, however. For the new believers it causes deep feelings of joy and nostalgia, but it also causes a severe confrontation with their families and former friends. Even though it has the blessing of apostolic precedence, the evangelist needs to remember that the burning of the Ephesian books precipitated a riot and nearly cost Gaius and Aristarchus their lives. There is nothing more offensive to a people than to see its religious objects going up in smoke at the hands of its adversaries. Christian congregations need to benefit from the destruction of past reverences, but they should not make public demonstrations of such burnings unless they are prepared to cope with the wrath of the community.

The missionary must remember that he is primarily a herald of a heavenly message, sent to gain converts, not to fight other religions. His identification with the culture in which he works is similar to the incarnation of Jesus Christ—he is truly a part of the cultural setting, but his purpose is to introduce constructive change and make disciples. He is a critic of moral ethics, a teacher of divine truth, an agitator of Christian action, an inciter of popular lay movements. He uses the reactions of the opposition to advance his own cause, so that whatever course the existing religions take he will gain benefit for his developing church. Once the Christian community begins to grow rapidly, anything the religious leaders do will force some people to make a choice, thus further creating an atmosphere for convert-making and spontaneous evangelism. The missionary's only defense for such behavior is the knowledge that Jesus Christ is the only true Savior and that all other religions fall short of eternal life.

It is important that a church avoid any major confrontations with the dominant local religion until it has attained (1) a large enough following to survive the conflict, (2) a sufficient number of sympathizers among the non-Christians to gain at least a measure of public support, (3) a favorable rapport with area officials of different levels of authority, and (4) a legal status, if possible, in the country.

The churches should not initiate confrontations with resisting religious groups, except through their normal range of evangelistic activities, but they do need to be ready for trouble when it comes. It is in the very nature of the Church and its claims that true Christians should not seek persecution for its own sake nor attempt to prod non-Christians into taking violent defensive action. Evangelical Christians should go about their normal ministries of proclaiming the gospel, teaching the doctrines and practices of the New Testament, and praying for all those who seek help from God. If persecution comes, the blood of the martyrs will still be the seed of the Church; but the Christian community should not go about asking for violence.

The Church must be militant, active, ever expanding over the face of the earth in spite of all opposition. The idea of total evangelization of necessity includes the inevitability of fierce confrontations with the religions that Christianity seeks to replace. At times there may even be some hostility from the nonevangelistic Christian groups. The world is not only ignorant of the true nature of Christ and His gospel; it has already committed itself to a great variety of alternate courses. Men will not leave those courses without a struggle, and some will not leave them at all. It is not the responsibility of the Church to convert the whole world, but to give every man a fair opportunity to understand the gospel and turn to Christ.

Paul was tempted to join the confrontation and defend the faith, especially when two of his workers were captured and in danger of their lives; but he yielded to the good sense of his fellow Christians and cooperated with the governmental authorities. The Christian community must never return evil for evil, even when believers are arrested or martyred. The Christian response must be one of love, leaving the meting of judgment in the hands of God. By neither overreacting nor giving any ground, the Church can ride through any persecution and ultimately prevail. In the end, the opposition will only serve to further polarize the opinions of the community and cause some previously unconvinced people to convert to Christianity.

Tremendous problems occur if the churches do not meet the confrontation with the world correctly. If premature, a fledgling church can be destroyed. If the church meets mob with mob, the future witness of the Christian community may be impaired. If the church fears the conflict too much, it will retreat from battle and cease to conquer. Jesus said in His Sermon on the Mount, "Blessed are they which are persecuted for righteousness' sake: for theirs is the kingdom of heaven. Blessed are ye, when men shall revile you, and persecute you, and shall say all manner of evil against you falsely, for my sake. Rejoice, and be exceeding glad: for great is your reward in heaven" (Matthew 5:10–12). He also said, "In the world ye shall have tribulation: but be of good cheer; I have overcome the world" (John 16:33).

As Paul yielded to good sense, missionaries should follow the instructions and advice of their congregations and the local authorities—short of withdrawal of the churches from occupied territory or making any unwise promises to limit evangelization. In many cases, persecution occurs in conjunction with some religious event and soon passes. At such times, the leaders of opposing religions feel obligated to make a public showing of their successful control over the rising threat of Christianity. It is often best on such occasions to avoid public confrontation, particularly if the event is marked by much drinking and abnormal behavior.

Paul and the Ephesian Christians survived the uprising at the amphitheater because they offered no immediate opposition. If Paul had tried to defend the faith on that day, he and the entire Christian community at Ephesus might well have been killed. They would have been recorded as martyrs, but they would have died unnecessarily in a battle they had already won.

Sometimes persecution accompanies political strife such as an election, a civil war, or any change of government leadership. Christ did not send His missionaries to die in civil uprisings. Whenever political violence breaks out, the missionaries should follow the instructions of their nation's embassy and withdraw from public life until the violence has run its course. The national church cannot keep its members from forming political opinions and becoming involved in the social controversies, but Christians must remember that their primary task takes precedence over any earthly movement and that they must still maintain their Christian testimony both during and after the conflict. One of the ironies of evangelization is that the Church will often grow very rapidly in the period immediately following a civil disruption, for the people are socially unsettled and often temporarily disillusioned with the forces that normally oppose the Church.

In the light of the militant attack of the Church on the non-Christian religions, one might well ask why countries allow missionaries inside their borders. In most countries the constitution calls for religious liberty, thus making it difficult to deny the entrance of religious teachers. There are many antiproselytization laws, but most of them are impossible to enforce. The situation is complicated by the factor that most political leaders are more interested in law and order than in the spiritual culture of their people. Often they like a competing minority religion to reduce the authority of the major religious group whose leaders seek to dominate them. Some governments want missionaries to assist with the education of their children and generally raise the living standards of their countries. Few nations would have advanced to their present standards if it had not been for the influence and work of missionaries.

There is yet another factor that allows missionaries to work in even some unreceptive countries. The alternatives are worse than letting the missionaries in. A government must never underestimate the evangelistic drive of the Christian faith. Where there is a door that is closed to the gospel, the Church will come over the walls and revert to secretive methods that offer a great popular appeal, especially among the people who may oppose the government. As a general rule, the Church will grow fastest in those areas that offer the most opposition.

The divine imperative to go into all the world and preach the gospel to every creature must take precedence over all human laws and regulations. Where Christian evangelization can be carried out legally, the churches must follow the biblical command, "Let every soul be subject unto the higher powers" (Romans 13:1); but, wherever the evangelical churches are denied entrance or seriously limited in their divinely ordered task, they must follow the example of the apostolic Church in the Roman empire and work illegally, no matter what the consequences. The Church has always thrived under the most difficult circumstances; it is public apathy that most seriously retards the development of the Church.

There are times when the Christian community must finally fight back, although always with methods that further the kingdom of God and allow the believers to attack on their own terms. The Church must be slow to anger, but when her anger is aroused she must be deliberate and efficient, even in her wrath displaying the finest qualities of the Christian faith.

In the Colombian town of Jenesano there lived only one evangelical Christian family. The religious leaders of the town were furious and threatened to burn the family's house if they did not leave the region. Complaints to the local police availed nothing, even though the priest declared over loudspeakers that "the Protestant plague has come!" Other nearby towns began to echo the threats. Early one Saturday morning we struck the town with six crowded busloads of our most fervent and best-trained evangelical witnesses. Armed with Bibles and thousands of pieces of gospel literature, they poured out of the buses and scattered throughout the town to hold street meetings on every corner.

The local people ran for their houses, expecting the same kind of violence they had threatened to employ; but when their curiosity brought them back to their windows they heard the sound of preaching the gospel of Christ. Crowds began to gather around the street meetings, the people moved to respect by the boldness of our action and the impressiveness of our numbers. By evening we had rented a house for a church location and had a new congregation of more than sixty believers. Such counterattacks should be rare, but they are occasionally necessary.

An active, evangelizing church will suffer persecution. It is unavoidable. Once a church passes through the throes of a strong siege of persecution, it becomes a stronger force in the community and gains more converts than in its prepersecution days. Opposition makes Christians firm in their faith, as hard work strengthens muscle fiber.

In the end, the churches benefit from persecution. The opposition of an idea only polarizes the public and causes more people to convert to it.

In the Kingdom of Tonga, for example, the entrance of an apostolically oriented church was strongly opposed by local people, but the opposition only brought it to the attention of the king, who honored the movement by cutting the ribbon to dedicate its new church building.

I was once arrested for preaching in the South American town of Miraflores, where we had made some thirty converts in one day. While under arrest, we won two of our jailers to the Lord and that night had another service with more conversions. The event caused such a stir in the Lengupa River Valley that the church grew very rapidly after that and was able to move its church building into the heart of the town.

The Church thrives in an atmosphere of conflict. When the social order is upset and religious powers are pressed out of their normal balance, the evangelical Christians can rise to their highest call to duty and make the sort of rapid gains necessary for a total world witness. If the blood of the martyrs is the seed of the Church, then social turmoil is its most fertile field and stormy conflict its life-giving rain.

10. The Emergence of a Missionary Church

PRINCIPLE: *The only way the world can be won for Christ is for every believer to be an evangelistic witness and for every church to become a center of missionary activity.*

The church that grew out of Ephesus became an evangelistic movement that thoroughly pervaded its own province with the gospel and spread the message of Christ along the busy trade routes for many hundreds of miles. The heavily populated Province of Asia—made up of the older regions of Mysia, Lydia, Caria, and Asian Phrygia—was some 250 miles wide by about the same distance north and south, yet within only two years "all they which dwelt in Asia heard the word of the Lord Jesus."

To the east was the well-evangelized Province of Galatia, which Paul had visited several times. Paul was to address one of his most beautiful epistles to the Galatians, and he would write another to the nearby Colossians. The gospel must have spread rapidly, fanning out along the Roman roads into Cappadocia, Cilicia, Syria, Armenia, and even farther eastward into Parthia and distant India. By the end of the century, the Provinces of Bithynia and Pontus would have so many Christians that the temples would be in disuse.

The churches could grow without limitation, for every Christian house was a potential meeting place. Rich or poor, Jew or Greek, Asian or Galatian could accept the gospel and worship among those of his own culture, language, or economic status. A Christian community was as apt to spring up in a country hamlet as in a city, as common in the elaborate country villas of the rich as in the crowded apartment houses of the lower classes. There were doubtlessly hundreds of Christian meeting places in the province, each of them a potential point from which other churches could be born.

Paul's ministry was not limited to Asia during this time, for he also carried on a continued communication with his churches in Macedonia and Achaia. He wrote an early letter to the Corinthians, which was subsequently lost. In his next letter to them, which we call First Corinthians, he said, "I wrote you in an epistle not to company with fornicators, . . . covetous, or extortioners, or with idolaters" (I Corinthians 5:9–11). He then went on to correct what he said in his first letter, explaining that he did not mean that they were not to associate with sinners, but that they were not to keep close company with unfaithful members who fell into sin. It is interesting to note that a letter Paul later had to correct never found its way into the canon of Holy Writ.

Also in his First Epistle to the Corinthians, Paul said that Apollos had joined him at Ephesus (I Corinthians 16:12). Three of the Corinthian brethren—Stephanas, Fortunatus, and Achaicus—came to Ephesus with an offering for Paul's ministry (I Corinthians 16:17–18). Another interesting visitor to Ephesus was Sosthenes, the former chief ruler of the Corinthian synagogue, who had taken Paul before Gallio, the Roman proconsul. By the time Paul wrote First Corinthians, Sosthenes was a converted believer, for Paul wrote, "Paul, called to be an apostle of Jesus Christ . . . and Sosthenes our brother" (I Corinthians 1:1).

In the spring of A.D. 56, Paul "sent into Macedonia . . . Timotheus and Erastus" (Acts 19:22). Timothy may have gone as far as Corinth, for Paul told the Corinthians, "Now if Timotheus come, see that he may be with you without fear" (I Corinthians 16:10). Paul began his own journey to those provinces in late May, for he also told the Corinthians, "I will tarry at Ephesus until Pentecost" (I Corinthians 16:8). It was about that time that the riot occurred during the Artemis Festival, for Luke wrote, "And after the uproar was ceased, Paul called unto him the disciples, and embraced them, and departed for to go into Macedonia" (Acts 20:1).

Paul had written the First Epistle to the Corinthians from Ephesus just before the riot and before he had sent Timothy and Erastus to Macedonia. He sent the letter to Corinth with Titus and another believer, for he told the Corinthians in his next letter to them, which he wrote from Macedonia, "I desired Titus, and with him I sent a brother" (II Corinthians 12:18). On his trip from Ephesus to Philippi, Paul was disturbed at not finding Titus waiting for him at Troas. Titus was supposed to have delivered First Corinthians and then traveled to Troas to bring Paul a report. Paul therefore said in his second epistle, "Furthermore, when I came to Troas to preach Christ's gospel . . . I had no rest in my spirit, because I found not Titus my brother: but taking my leave of them, I went from thence into Macedonia" (II Corinthians 2:12–13).

The evidence proves that Paul did not limit himself to the Province of Asia while he lived in Ephesus. Even while he was so busily engaged in local ministry in Asia, he carried on other ministries in a wider and wider circle of missionary influence and vision.

As the initial phase of the Asian church came to an end, Paul did not confuse the nationalization of the work with the end of his own missionary career. He still had before him many years of working among the churches all through Asia Minor, Macedonia, Crete, Greece, Italy, and perhaps even to Spain. He would continue to carry on a very active literature ministry, eventually resulting in much of our New Testament. He would spend several years in prison in Caesarea and Rome; but, in the opinion of the author, he would be released again and do considerable missionary travel and work before his last arrest and martyrdom in Rome.

The Asian churches, too, were to continue their active work and to remain important missionary centers with a vision for the whole world. The earliest Christian missionaries into what is now France went out from Polycarp's church in Smyrna. Pothinus was the first missionary from Asia to southern Gaul. Later Irenaeus was sent out to join him. When Pothinus was martyred, Iranaeus carried on the work at Lyons and through his writings saved the believers in Rome and the whole Western Church from crumbling under the Montanist and Valentinian heresies. Ultimately, it was Paul's missionary church in Asia, not that of Rome, that became the mother and doctrinal guardian of the Church throughout the first two Christian centuries.

A church produced by correct missionary principles will in turn produce more missionaries and missionary churches. The enormity of the task demands that every member be mobilized for missions, every church be developed into a center for world evangelization. Unless new churches can be oriented to apostolic values and old churches be transformed into evangelistic centers, there is little hope that the Christian faith will ever gain on the enormous multiplication of human beings in the world. The mathematical factors of the demographic explosion place world evangelization beyond the reach of token efforts at missions or the halfhearted dedication of many of today's churches.

Yet the Church can attain a state of numerical expansion if apostolically minded pastors will motivate their people and if all Bible-believing Christians will allow themselves to be mobilized for this divine task. There are enough millions of Christian people in the world that the Great Commission could be attainable, if the drive for total evangelization would become a fresh movement among evangelical churches. All the factors for success are present; there lacks only a sufficient number of inspired people to comprehend the need and speak the movement into being.

The mathematical increase in the world's population must be matched and surpassed by the evangelistic mission of the Church. This will require a dedication approaching fanaticism on the part of Christian leaders and a total mobilization for missionary evangelism on the part of the Bible-believing churches.

In trying to figure out how the tiny atom could be converted into an explosive source of energy, Albert Einstein created the now famous formula $E = mc^2$—that the energy produced by releasing any of the particles of an atom is equal to the mass of the atomic particle times the square of the speed of light. An atomic particle is incomprehensively small, but the speed of light is 186,300 miles per second. The square of the speed of light is 186,300 times 186,300, or 34,707,690,000! In spite of its insignificant size, when the mass of an atomic particle is multiplied by a figure like that it can destroy a city and threaten a world.

The formula $E = mc^2$ can also be applied to world evangelization, although with a different definition. In this case, $E = mc^2$ means:

EVANGELIZATION equals . . . the number of gospel-preaching MINISTERS times the ideal size of an apostolic-type CONGREGATION, SQUARED.

Church growth cannot really be reduced to a mathematical formula because there are too many variables, but it is interesting to see how this particular formula illustrates how the world could be evangelized.

Let us set the world's population at a temporary 4 billion. In most Protestant denominations the number of credentialed ministers is about one-half of 1 percent of the total number of members and adherents in regular attendance. As an example, one major church with a foreign constituency of 3,150,000 has 17,100 national workers with some kind of ministerial credentials, which comes to .0054, or .5 percent. At the present time, the Protestant churches make up only about 8 percent of the world's population, or about 320 million constituents. One-half of 1 percent of that figure would be 1.6 million ministers.

Following the idea that the modern churches ought to return to the apostolic concept of scattering smaller congregations in homes all through the community and using their central facilities more for Christian education and evangelistic rallies, we will arbitrarily set the average attendance in such home meetings at fifty. If the average attendance would be less, then the number of ministers in relation to the total constituency would need to increase proportionately. The size of the apostolic-type congregation squared would be 50 times 50, or 2,500.

The solution to the missions formula $E = mc^2$ is as follows: the total evangelization of 4 billion people is equal to the number of ministers (1.6 million) multiplied by the size of apostolic-type congregations squared (2,500). That is, 4 billion equals 1.6 million times 2,500. What this means is that the average gospel worker must evangelize not a world of 4 billion people but a much more reachable number of 2,500.

This formula merely provides an example of how the task of world evangelization could be completed rapidly if the entire Protestant church were mobilized along the lines of apostolic Christianity. The formula (any population figure $\times$ .08 $\times$ .005 $\times$ 50^2 = the total beginning number) works only if the Protestant church makes up 8 percent of the population, the ministers and other gospel workers make up one-half of 1 percent of the members and adherents, and the average size of an apostolic-type congregation would be 50 persons. If any of the factors were altered, the formula would require other changes to maintain the desired result of total saturation of the beginning population. However, the same may be said of the condition illustrated by the formula. If the percentage of Christian believers decreases, then the Church must respond with an increase in its number of dedicated witnesses to regain any lost ground and ultimately to surpass the percentage of population growth. As the Church gains on the population and increases its number of witnesses, the remaining responsibility of each local congregation will theoretically diminish until the necessary church size will reduce from fifty to the presently unthinkable number of one. At that point, all the world would be evangelized and in church.

Even though one can dream mathematically of the total Christianization of the world, the goal is total evangelization not total Christianization. Each congregational leader does not have to convert 2,500 people. What he has to do is mobilize his community of believers to take the gospel effectively to those people so that every man, woman, and child hears a·clear explanation of the gospel, has a fair chance to accept or reject Jesus Christ as his Savior and Lord, and has a continuing opportunity to worship God in an apostolically oriented congregation of Christian believers.

The problem becomes one of establishing strategic locations for evangelical workers and their mobilized congregations. As long as the great majority of apostolically oriented Christians are concentrated in the Anglo-Scandinavian cultures, there can be no mathematical chance of world evangelization. This means that the churches must radically expand their foreign mission programs to spread their ministers and laymen all over the earth in a more practical distribution of contact points with the population. The Bible-believing Church must actively proclaim the gospel wherever men live, no matter what the cultural, racial, linguistic, geographical, or governmental difficulties encountered. The Church must become evenly distributed over the earth's population.

To reach the world will require a much stronger missionary commitment. Christians at all levels of authority or position must be mobilized for an all-out pervasion of society with a positive Christian witness. Like produces like, so Christians must pervade society until the Church grows of its own life in all cultures of every nation.

Will there always be a need for the traditional missionary? If by traditional we mean a paternalistic egotist who goes from his favored position in a dominant culture to civilize and Christianize the culturally deprived, the answer is a definite No. The world does not need him now; it did not need him in the past. Yet the notoriety of such missionaries has overshadowed the fact that they have always been in the minority. Most missionaries are sincerely dedicated people who lack only the right concepts to put together a winning combination of missions development. Many are already applying apostolic principles on their fields.

There will always be a tragic disparity between the challenge of the fields and the availability of sufficiently trained and motivated laborers to bring in the harvest. The larger the Church grows, the greater will be the need for qualified assistance between countries, both in finances and in personnel. If missionaries insist on remaining in charge of activities that rightfully belong to the local and national churches, then they will some day be out of a job; but if they remain at the cutting edge of world evangelism and help the churches to grow without disparaging the worth or the capabilities of the believers, they will be in considerably more demand than they can ever fulfill.

If the missionary seeks to do only the pioneer type of work in establishing new churches in unevangelized territory, he may find that the national church will grow right past him and leave him with churches that do not fit the national pattern or its personality. If he withdraws from the national church, he will only fragment the church and divide its momentum. On the other hand, if he stays in the national church and competes with national leaders for its available positions, he will some day be driven away by the very people he first went to save. There is really only one sensible solution: the missionary must work in cooperation with the national church, remaining in the front lines of evangelism without becoming either a threat or a hindrance to the growing community of Christian believers, and remaining mobile enough to adapt quickly to new challenges, new conditions, and new locations.

The condition of some missionaries is like that of a carpenter who fell in love with his hammer. At first, he marveled over the powerful blow he could strike with a single blow of his well-balanced tool, but as time went on he began to worry about the scratches he was putting in the instrument. In his forceful use of the hammer he had sometimes missed the mark, and those mistakes had caused irreparable damage to the sides of the beautiful steel head. So he began to ease up a bit when he hit those rough nails. As time went on, he would clean his hammer every night and polish it until it glistened. He would take his hammer out of its wrappings and stand on the job for hours just looking at it and thinking of the many houses it had built over the years. With his own hands and the gentle tappings of his beloved hammer he built a special carrying case for the instrument and lined it with plush velvet. How proudly he carried it, and how hushed became his voice whenever he spoke of his tool's glorious past. Finally, he had the hammer gold-plated and hung it reverently over the mantle of his fireplace. Now he sits in his favorite rocker and gazes at his inactive hammer, while twilight turns to night and the embers die in the fireplace.

Missionaries, too, can forget what they started out to do. Even the mistakes of missionaries have ways of becoming hallowed traditions that linger on to haunt many a fireplace. The most deadly of missionary mistakes occur when a missionary forgets his calling and becomes more concerned with his daily routine than with the original purpose of his schedule. Once a missionary ceases to be a fervent agitator for religious change, he may continue to occupy his pedestal of missionary honor, but he is no longer a practical tool for world evangelization.

The missionary of the future must allow the national church to develop its own personality without interference. He must move men by his dynamic ministry, not by usurping authority not rightfully his. Even if he is the father of the work, he must not act as though the believers are his children. The future successful missionary will be a catalyst who causes things to happen without being himself a part of the event. He will continuously incite the atmosphere for church growth and the development of national believers and leaders, while keeping himself in the sociocultural background. He will be a mover of men, an inciter of mass action, a teacher of truth to those who will take the truth to their world. He will be a man whom the national believers love and respect, whose ideas they follow without following the man, and whose spirit they imbibe for strength to face their society with the claims of Jesus Christ. Such men will be rare, but their relative scarcity will only add to their effectiveness by making their ministries more valuable to the national churches.

As national churches continue to develop, more and more countries will send out their missionaries to evangelize unreached and difficult areas. The work of missionaries will become less Western and more cooperative, with the brothers of many nations joining shoulder to shoulder in the common battle for the minds and souls of men. This is already beginning to happen, and it is beautiful to behold.

It will take the concerted efforts of evangelical believers in every church in every nation to come anywhere near the fulfillment of the awesome Great Commission. As time goes on and national churches develop into responsible maturity, the role of the foreign missionary changes but it does not end. Those missionaries with the creative insight to envision their next steps toward the completion of their holy task, and who take those steps decisively and with courage within the setting of a rising complex of national churches, will find a lifetime career of rewarding Christian service.

The role of the missionary is to teach the Christian believers of each nation to evangelize their own people and to incite in each country the conditions in which will occur spontaneous movements of church growth.

11. The Ephesian Method at Work

PRINCIPLE: *The only kind of Christianity that can evangelize the world is that which returns to the standards and the missionary methods of the apostolic Church.*

The candlestick that illuminated all of Asia no longer sheds its light on Ephesus. The pilgrim to the Turkish town of Selchuk sees only the scattered ruins of a once proud and influential city, its broken columns lying like the whitened bones of some prehistoric creature whose fossilized remains offer little more than a hint of the magnificent life that once thrived there.

Even the sea has departed. The Aegean is only distantly visible from the ruins of Ephesus now. Thousands of years of erosion in the Galatian highlands have deposited great volumes of silt in the Cayster River's bed and moved its mouth farther out to sea. The ships stopped coming to Ephesus, and the commerce ceased to flow along her roads. As the trade shifted to other ports, the light of the city flickered and died.

The ruins of the old Temple of Artemis lie quietly now, giving little indication of their former glory. The world's largest building, where men gathered to seek the fertility of their enterprises, now is a heap of rubble in a very unfertile place that in the rainy season becomes a swamp. The beautiful amphitheater is still there, but the pale relics that once echoed to the shouts of "Great is Artemis of the Ephesians" now hear only the patter of rain and the mournful lamentation of the Aegean winds.

The man who bore the torch of Christianity to Ephesus finally was beheaded for his fierce dedication to the cause he preached among these ruins. The men who worked with him scattered over the empire to preach the gospel in other cities with the same evangelistic fervor. They challenged the very stronghold of Asian heathenism, and when the battle was over they moved on to wage other battles on other grounds.

To stand and look upon the remains of Ephesus now, the knowledgeable visitor feels a surging wave of nostalgia for the glory that is departed. Old Ephesus is gone, and with her died all the things she deemed important enough to fight for. Alas, she is survived by her most serious foe—for the Church she so opposed still lives in victorious good health, still pressing onward and threatening to plant the cross in every community on the face of the earth.

The living remains of Ephesus are not to be found among her crumbled ruins, but in the results of the evangelistic campaign that once shook her society and established the Church of Jesus Christ firmly in the middle of the Roman empire. The letter Paul wrote at Ephesus and sent to Corinth by the hands of Titus became a part of the Christian New Testament; and the story Luke recorded in the Acts of the Apostles still lives along with the divine cause that brought those memorable events to pass.

The Church must look to Ephesus again and remember. In its quest for a workable evangelistic method for its confrontation with the twentieth-century world, it must turn its eyes back to Ephesus and pick up again those missionary principles first established there. The forgotten sword buried so long among the relics of Ephesus will still fit the hand of a militantly evangelistic Church and cut through the defenses of heathenism to conquer the world for Jesus Christ.

The method of the apostle Paul at Ephesus is still a workable plan of world evangelization, for no other system has ever produced the total results that Paul and his team attained in their Asian campaign. The set of missionary principles employed there thoroughly evangelized the Province of Asia, and they will work in the same way today if missionaries will apply them with apostolic dedication.

One cannot say that there is anything new or revolutionary in any of the principles themselves. It is, rather, the particular combination of factors in their original sequence that makes the plan unique. The reason they have seldom reappeared in church history is that the Church has seldom dedicated itself to this kind of total evangelization. During the greater part of Christian history, the Church has relied too heavily upon its domination by political and military force and too little on the power of its heavenly message to transform human lives. Even after missionaries began to go out beyond the protective circles of their own nations' domains, they seemed afraid to trust the apostolic methods. They substituted the power of preaching with a wide range of charitable institutions. When at last some mission societies began to proclaim the message of personal salvation, much of today's missionary work had already been initiated. Now it is long overdue that the Church return to the evangelistic methods of the first-century Church and apply those principles in an apostolic pattern.

The most serious deterent to this Ephesian method of missions has been the lack of any unified missionary philosophy. Written instructions to missionaries emphasize financial policies and organizational structures, generally settling for a brief statement of purpose about the fulfillment of the Great Commission, but seldom defining a method of working that could unite the missionary forces into an effective team and assure evangelistic success. This tendency to send missionaries to remote parts of the earth without definite job descriptions has led to a wide variety of methods and caused most missionaries to become strong individualists. American missionaries particularly have carried with them the competitive traits that characterize Protestant ministry in the United States. The environment on most mission fields has not been conducive to the spontaneous development of teamwork that the apostolic example demands.

The same problem that has discouraged the rise of apostolic methods in the past can frustrate their success in the future if missionaries do not voluntarily unite their efforts and if mission boards do not orient their staffs to more cooperative ways of working overseas. In much the same manner, this applies to pastors who wish to put the Ephesian method into operation. Churches and their pastors will have to stop competing with one another and choose to unite their efforts against the common enemies of church growth.

The Ephesian method is so easily understood and based on plain good sense that its chief mystery is why it has not been more widely accepted in the Church, after such a spectacular application in the first century. Perhaps the answer is that it must be totally comprehended to work at all. Its only real secret is that it requires the whole method in its entirety for any of its parts to work effectively. The accumulated effect of the whole method is something much more than the sum of the results of its single compenents—as a cake is more than the sum of its ingredients. Mass evangelism alone is little more than a religious circus. Church-establishing without training gospel workers for practical ministry leads to the paternalistic domination of foreign missionaries. Confronting the major forces of a heathen society without first forming a solid base of local support leads to disaster. It is the aggregated total of the apostolic principles combined in a particular sequence and applied in their en-tirety that makes the Ephesian method so irresistibly successful. Best of all, it has the blessing of biblical precedence.

The Ephesian method of missions can be applied with understandable variations in any culture on earth. Local regulations may limit certain kinds of mass evangelization, but otherwise the method will remain constant. No one can predict when the opposition of non-Christian forces will come, but the Church should pray that it be allowed to form its base before it is made to confront its opponent on a major scale. Minor resistance along the way will only strengthen the fledgling church and prepare it for the greater battle to come. Wherever possible, mis-sionaries should seek to follow the method in its apostolic order, leaving out none of the steps along the way. In places already committed to other philosophies, the leaders will need to get together to discuss how they can take advantage of what they have already accomplished and eliminate or at least isolate the activities that will detract from the new method.

In some cases, missionaries will say that they have already used these same principles and failed to get the promised effect. The Ephesian method can be carried out to the letter without developing the spontaneous lay movements required for total world evangelization. This could be caused by an error at any stage, particularly in the original strategy, the choice of a vital location, or in the formation of the beginning nucleus of believers. The situation is like some strings of Christmas-tree lights—if one bulb fails, the whole string refuses to light up. Even more important than any of the parts of the plan is the choice of missionary personnel to carry out the method and their degree of dedication to the cause of Christ. The apostle Paul demonstrated repeatedly that he was willing even to die for the evangelization of the world, and it is doubtful that any less inspired effort will accomplish similar results in our times.

The Ephesian method is difficult, and the task it undertakes to accomplish is next to impossible. Yet if missionaries will put it into practice one phase at a time, accompanying their work with a fervent passion for its success, they can see it work as well as it did the first time. Missionaries will have to adapt the method to each country, as Paul himself did, but the principles will remain the same.

The Ephesian method, then, is as follows:

1. *A Single Purpose:* Underlying all evangelistic activities there must be a unified, cooperative agreement that the primary task of the Church is to fulfill the Great Commission. The Church will not have completed that original assignment until every man, woman, and child on the face of the earth shall have had a fair chance to understand the significance of the gospel, had an opportunity to accept or reject Jesus Christ as his Savior and Lord, and had the continued prospect of worshiping God in a community of Christian believers.

The primary purpose of Jesus Christ in the world must never become a secondary cause in His Church.

2. *Preliminary Planning:* Before missionary activities are initiated in a country, the mission board and the missionaries must thoroughly research the proposed field and choose strategic locations for their vital evangelistic centers. When a national church is involved, the same principle applies that all major moves should be part of a total plan.

Particular care should be given to the patterns of social movement so that the natural flow of population will carry the gospel where the evangelists want it to go.

Evangelization on a worldwide scale requires preliminary planning and careful strategy. The planning is as critical as the execution in reaching the world for Christ.

3. *Cooperative Teamwork:* It is impossible for single individual efforts to reach the world for Christ. Missionaries must unite their activities into cooperative teamwork of interdependent ministries, setting aside all competitiveness with one another in favor of presenting a unified front to the real enemies of church growth.

The apostolic pattern of evangelism requires the teamwork of dedicated people laboring effectively toward a single predetermined goal.

4. *A Basic Nucleus:* Because the masses are irrational and respond only affirmatively or negatively to symbolic images, individual prospects should first be attracted to a basic nucleus of believers who represent in microcosm what the church is to be when it is grown. Nothing vital should be left out of the preparation of these first believers, for they should exhibit the whole spectrum of apostolic doctrine, religious experience, fundamental practices, and basic priorities.

Before an evangelist can take the gospel to the masses, he must first form a nucleus of properly oriented believers with whom the new converts may identify.

5. *Mass Communications:* One-to-one witnessing is certainly to be encouraged, but the Church will never reach the whole world without mass evangelism. Somehow the gospel must be communicated to large numbers of people to the point that it becomes an issue in the community. Mass evangelism is most effective when it is operated in a cycle of drawing prospective believers from the masses, assimilating them into the churches, and returning to the masses again for another group of prospects.

To evangelize large numbers of people, the missionary must somehow bring his message to the attention of the public and break down the masses into workable groups of favorable individual contacts.

6. *Establish Congregations:* The previous stages of the method are all aimed at preparation for the major task of establishing communities of Christian believers in thriving congregations. The Church of Jesus Christ exists in its entirety wherever it is manifested, beginning with two or three believers gathered together. It is in the very nature of the Christian experience to desire to join together in churches.

Effective mass evangelization always requires that the resulting converts be established in responsible Christian congregations.

7. *Trained National Leaders:* There will never be enough foreign missionaries to evangelize the whole earth. The only way the world can be reached is for the missionaries to teach the people of each country to evangelize their own people and to incite the conditions in which spontaneous lay movements of church expansion will occur. The teaching of pastors and other church leaders must be on a practical level that best trains them and motivates them for fervent service.

If church growth is to result from massive lay movements, it is essential that the people of each country be taught to pastor their own churches, lead their own evangelistic programs, and direct their own national organizations.

8. *Maintain Momentum:* The natural tendency of a movement is to grow by stages, the phases of rapid expansion coming farther and farther apart until growth becomes insignificant. The missionary cannot allow this to happen to his evangelistic movement, because his goal is total evangelization. He maintains momentum through a vision for continuous growth, the constant development of fresh leadership, a realistic method of financing his operations, and the application of the New Testament ministries of preaching, teaching, and believing for miracles.

The success of world missions is not to be measured against past accomplishments or present gains, but by the fulfillment of the total claims of the Great Commission and the response of the Church to plan and maintain a missionary vision.

9. *Overcome Opposition:* Sooner or later, an attempt at total world evangelization must come into life-or-death struggles with the other religions and philosophies of the planet. The Church must be sure to

establish a strong base of believers and sympathizers before serious confrontations occur; otherwise it may find itself outnumbered and outmaneuvered. The Church must not purposely initiate a violent confrontation, neither should it return violence for violence. The Church cannot be stopped by opposition, for only social acceptance can control it.

When the growing Christian community becomes large enough to be a force in the society, its evangelistic action will provoke a responding counteraction from the major religions of the area. This often occurs when the economy and balance of power are most seriously effected.

10. *A Missionary Church:* Churches begun on sound missionary principles will themselves become missionary-minded congregations who will share in the concepts of world evangelization and cooperate in the cause. As national churches become increasingly evangelistic in their outlook and practice, missionaries can branch out into other supporting tasks to increase the depth of the evangelistic channel and expand the flow of new converts into the Church.

The only way the world can possibly be won for Christ is for every believer to be an evangelistic witness and for every church to become a center for missionary activity.

This is the Ephesian method of missions.

Add to these working principles the factor of an expanding number of Christian witnesses, pledged to the death to plant the cross of Jesus Christ in every community on the face of the earth, and there is no power that can stop its spontaneous progress.

Many evangelical groups will not accept the Ephesian method— some of them out of irreversible commitments to their own traditional conservativism, and others out of fear or mere inertia—but others will awaken to the original concepts of apostolic evangelism and revolutionize their missionary practices. They will exchange their more recent medieval, Reformational, or Fundamentalistic traditions for the much older customs of apostolic missionary dedication that will liberate them from their stained-glass prisons as a butterfly bursts free from its cocoon.

There is a big world waiting outside the walls, if a church will dare to return to the apostolic principles of total world evangelization first laid down by the apostle Paul at Ephesus.